# THE DOG OF MEMORY

# THE DOG OF MEMORY

*A Family Album of Secrets and Silences*

## Alvin Greenberg

The University of Utah Press

*Salt Lake City*

07 06 05 04 03 02
5 4 3 2 1

LIBRARY OF CONGRESS CATALOGING-IN-PUBLICATION DATA
Greenberg, Alvin.
The dog of memory / Alvin Greenberg.
p.   cm.
ISBN 0-87480-727-1 (acid-free paper)
1. Greenberg, Alvin. 2. Greenberg, Alvin—Family.
3. Authors, American—20th century—Biography.
4. Authors, Ameican—20th century—Family relationships.
I. Title
PS3557.R377 D64 2002
818'.5409—dc21
2002003441

Excerpt from Robert Frost, "Mending Wall," in *The Poetry of Robert Frost,*
ed. Edward Connery Lathem. Copyright 1930, 1939, 1969 by Henry Holt
and Co., © 1958 by Robert Frost, © 1967 by Lesley Frost Ballantine.
Reprinted by permission of Henry Holt and Company, LLC.

The Defiance House Man colophon is a registered trademark of
The University of Utah Press. It is based upon a four-foot tall
Ancient Puebloan pictograph (late PIII) near Glen Canyon, Utah.

# CONTENTS

# ACKNOWLEDGMENTS

Several essays from this collection appeared previously in a slightly different form: "Remember the Alamo" *American Literary Review;* "Voices" and "Herb: A Memoir" in *The Antioch Review;* "The Ever-Present" and "Here and There" in *Ascent;* "The Music of Silence" in *Georgia Review;* "The Dog of Memory" in *Graywolf Forum Three: The Business of Memory;* and an extract from "Shirts and Skins" in *The Hungry Mind Review.*

I'd like to thank the editors of the above journals, where some of these essays first appeared; Dawn Marano of the University of Utah Press, whose editorial advice has been consistently thoughtful, generous, and helpful; and my wife, Janet Holmes, whose support throughout this project—and our life together—has been so wonderful.

# THE DOG OF MEMORY

# WHAT STREAMS THROUGH US

"Childhood is not just what we recall from our own younger years," remarks one recent critic of the American passion for nostalgia in his riff on our dream of the past, "it is possibility itself, the fantasy of what is available." But in fact I lived those fantasies Sven Birkerts, in "American Nostalgia," then fashions into clichés. I had that very childhood that he dismisses as only a vision of possibility—a very ordinary childhood, as I've always thought of it—and not just in the golden glow of nostalgia, either, but in its realities.

It didn't take place in one of the small, essentially rural towns the sort of nostalgia that this critic parodies generally takes us back to, but in a medium-size city, Cincinnati. We lived on what were then its outskirts, where our suburban neighborhood backed up against the industrial on one edge and the agricultural on another, a mix of suburban housing, cow pastures, and nearby chemical plants and railroads: where, in fact, we actually did chase fireflies and play kick-the-can on long, languid summer evenings till the voices of mothers began calling us home in the gathering dusk; where we wandered along the creek bed, capturing crawdads and frogs and each other in our Wild West games, unwatched and unsupervised, unbothered and ungoverned by any adults; where I played baseball on Saturday mornings, went to Granny's for lunch and to ten-cent movies in the afternoon; where my parents took us on long Sunday drives to nowhere in particular; where the neighbors really did all know one another, and we

walked to school, and the corner drugstore sold cherry phos-
phates and penny candies. True things, all of these, and none
of Norman Rockwell's doings whatsoever.

Of course, it's also true that the creek we played in and
around was so polluted—running acidic green one day, bilious
purple the next—that no sane and knowledgeable parent, had
any followed us down into that exotic landscape, would have
let children anywhere near it. And it's also true that the Ober-
meyer boys down at the far end of the block called me a dirty
Jew and sicced their dog (a German shepherd, what else!) on
me, sending me fleeing home in terror, outrunning that evil
Nazi beast—oh, I was the speediest kid in the neighborhood
back then—all the way up the back steps of our house to
where, just as I grabbed the doorknob, it sank its fangs into
my little ten-year-old butt. And it's also true that Bill Berkey,
the oldest kid in the neighborhood—all of twelve or thirteen
maybe—showed up with a .22 pistol one day and shot a blue
jay out of the Jamesons' elm tree and that in the schoolyard at
recess one day Donny McClanahan was stabbed in the belly
and doomed to a slow, painful recuperation.

And speaking of grade school, that's where I first met the
anti-intellectualism that I was later to learn is as crucial to
America's idea of itself as nostalgia for the fresh sweet corn my
father loved to sink his teeth into. Me, I was just a kid who'd
never had an idea in his limited life span and was mostly just
busy playing his way rather mindlessly through his childhood,
as he would have thought he was supposed to do if he had
been given to thinking about what he was doing instead of
just doing it. The error of my ways came down on me as hard
as one of our sudden summer thunderstorms, and with just as
much of a dampening effect, the moment the word got around
at the end of sixth grade that I had passed the citywide test
that would enable me to attend the elite college-prep com-
bined junior high and high school, rather than sticking it out

at the elementary through eighth grade and then moving on to the district high school. And, worse yet, that, in spite of the principle's dire warning that such an act would constitute a terrible betrayal, I had in fact decided to accept that option. I hadn't actually given it any thought. It just seemed as much the natural thing to do as meeting in the McCormicks' backyard for an afternoon pickup softball game, though from that moment on, until we moved from the neighborhood—which, fortunately, was not long after—those games weren't much fun for me. I was shunned. No one would pick me to play on his side, and though there wasn't any overt hostility or anti-Semitism involved, my academic choice had now lined all the kids up on the Obermeyers' side. If I went down by the creek that final summer we lived on Fenmore Drive, it was alone—or, worse yet, in either the ignominious company of my baby brother or that of the longtime neighborhood outcast, little Eddy Levy, whom even I didn't particularly want to be seen with.

The point of all this—or at least one of the points—is that what passes for nostalgia, which has been getting a bad rap these days, walks the world hand in hand with what passes for reality, though in my experience we're only talking about two kinds of reality: the benevolent and the malevolent. Either way, it's the stories we tell each other and ourselves that we love, especially these stories of our pasts. Perhaps the real gift of language is not its capacity to communicate information but the fact that we've evolved through it—fairly early in our history, I suspect—into the storytelling animal. Yet we are not, as some critics of memoir would have it, engaged in the dysfunctional confabulation that sometimes afflicts Alzheimer's patients, causing them to blurt out reports of events that never happened. Yes, we may view the past only darkly through the lenses of individual perception, and on occasion we may indeed, intentionally or otherwise, colorize its sometimes-grim grays with rose-colored glasses, but there are also plenty of times when it's not the glasses that are rose colored—or many hued, or shadowed, or aflame—but the very objects of our perception.

That nameless creek really did flow through the dreamscape that constituted the summer days of my childhood: it was the Africa where I swung Tarzan-like across its improbably colored waters on clothesline rope we had strung from overhanging branches, the Wild West where I lurked in the dense underbrush on the far shore with my twin six-shooter cap pistols, and the impassable Amazon when it flooded. What did we know of its carcinogenic potential back then? If I can trace my most pleasant childhood memories back to that little stream, can I also find the source of my bladder cancer there?

So what we have here is neither the simple reality that I can call up with a mix of bliss and bafflement nor the rancid mythologizing that others condemn, but something a little more complex than either. If there's a small voice in my mind still asking how they, my parents, could have been so negligent as to let me play around that open sewer of chemical contaminants, into which I splashed on a regular basis, groping for crawdads, there's also another that relishes the freedom I had to plunge into the world like that, something today's parents, far more conscious of the world's dangers, aren't likely to grant. And the polluted creeks, moreover, have long since been civilized: cleaned up and diverted into tunnels running under neighborhoods whose residents aren't even aware of their existence.

There was also one of those trickling along underneath my childhood, the usual rancid rivulet of family secrets, full of death, detritus, and disposal, almost motionless, but still managing to ooze along under every house we lived in, shaping the very ground I lived upon. Shaping me—without, of course, my knowing it. Signs of its presence, too subtle for me to understand, wicked upward from time to time, dampening the walls of my disposition, but I mistook that for my own soggy, shapeless interior and went on splashing across the surface of my life.

We're shaped not just by the quotidian life but also by the risks we've taken or been thrust—or stumbled—into, knowingly or not, that we carry forward into our later lives. I'm not talking about defining moments—the lightning bolt of the instant when you realize you've fallen in love, the thunderclap of your doctor's reporting that, yes, it is malignant—which seem to me to belong to another category altogether, the category of the life-changing event. My interest here is less with the things that change us than with the things that shape us. We may be knocked right off the slow-moving sidewalk of where we are by one of those defining moments, but how we got that far in the first place is a function of those shaping forces, and chief among them is memory: call it nostalgia if you must, but remember, it's grounded in the strange streams of reality that flow through our early life, including the risks they embody.

Once upon a time, at the far end of that toxic, meandering stream, or at least as far as a long day's outing with a bag lunch I'd made and packed myself (a hard-boiled egg and my all-time favorite, an onion sandwich) would take me, lost in a strange place midway through the journey of my childhood, I found myself in a waking nightmare. It doesn't seem likely that I would have made this journey alone, but I have no recollection of anyone being with me. The ground crunching underfoot was no longer the slippery shale and soft soil of the murky creek bed or its shrubby, overgrown banks but a dull, dry orange, the crumbled and hard-packed residue of coal fires (as I knew from the clinkers my father hauled out of the furnace once a week all winter long) that under the heat of the summer sun felt as if they were still capable of burning through my Keds.

And the world did indeed seem to be burning. All around me—as if only a moment before, wandering through the playground of my childhood, I had suddenly dropped through a hole in the earth into another world—huge mounds of smoldering garbage pyramided over me, high as houses, acrid fumes from slow-burning fires deep in their interiors spiraling upward into the noonday sun. Alleys of burnt cinders I didn't dare to enter ran among them, leading, I was sure, to yet more of these seething volcanoes. It was a fire-breathing dragon of a place, and I was spiked to the ground in front of it, not out of fear, surprisingly, but amazement, amazement that there could be such a place.

And then I saw them. Scabby old men in rags, mostly Negroes, as I thought of them then, but some white men as well, stared at me from out of the darkness inside the ramshackle hovels they'd constructed at the bases of these mountains of refuse, out of cardboard cartons and doorless refrigerators and hulks of burnt-out cars. Maybe there were half a dozen of them, maybe only two; I don't remember. It doesn't make any difference—one would have been enough. They stared at me—that they were aware of my presence I had no doubt—but they neither moved nor spoke. Nor did I. Nothing happened. We could have been statues, all of us, or, these days, an installation piece, "Untitled": make of it what you will, or consider what it might make of me.

I couldn't have stood there very long, however; the caustic smell, the burnt and bitter taste of those fires I knew must have been burning forever and would go on burning till the end of time, was seeping in through every sweaty pore of my childhood. I had been granted a glimpse of hell, and it was the riveting, wrenching place of nightmare, and nowhere I wanted to stay.

I never told a soul about this till now. Surely they must have asked me about my day when I got home, just the usual, vague where've-you-been and what've-you-been-doing sort of thing, and if so I would have answered—I was a good, obedient kid—with something equally vague, I'm sure. But maybe not. To the best of my recollection, no one paid any more attention to my comings and goings than they did to the infamous storm clouds gathering over Europe at the time, when they undoubtedly should have been keeping a close eye on both. I suppose one of the reasons I kept mum must have been my worry about what the adult response to learning where I'd been would be; at the very least, I'd be forbidden to go back there again. But the fact was, I didn't want to go back there again. I'd been there. I'd seen what I had seen, the likes of which I had never seen or imagined before. It was amazing, what the world contained, and now I had it contained within myself, and I wasn't about to let it out.

■

To follow the flow of water is to embark on a journey whose end you can't predict. I think of Huck and Jim, of Conrad's Marlowe, of Marc Antony on Cleopatra's barge, and of the people I keep reading about who tumble overboard and drown on, according to the experts, "safe" white-water rafting trips. I don't recall with any confidence whether my own travels were upstream like Marlowe's or downstream like Huck's—downstream, most likely, toward the Mill Creek Valley that served as the major drainage basin for Cincinnati's industrial waste in those days. I may have been on foot, but I was adrift, adrift in my own childhood as though it were a raft pushed out into the current to carry me through that part of my life. If the end was adulthood, I couldn't see that far, not around all the twists and bends coming up, the snags I'd be caught by and culverts I'd be flushed through and sandbars I'd find myself camping out on, the underground waters suddenly surfacing—wondering what the rest of the voyage held in store. It never even occurred to me to look, to wonder if there were any navigational maps, to ask if anyone else had ever been this way before.

If I'd been knowledgeable enough to name my vessel, I'd have called it *Thoughtless*.

No way in the world I could have known that these ordinary, fair-weather sailings of mine were the stuff of nostalgia-to-be, the craft carrying me toward who I would become. So far as I knew, it was a journey like any other. The shore was further off than I realized, and no one was watching (no one, I have come to suspect, is ever watching); I did what I did, and I let that doing take me where it would. Were it not for the fact that that journey came so curiously colored, its greens and reds and purples shifting from day to day, the acrid smoke of a reality even the tongue could taste wafting over it, some might say I dreamed my way through my childhood, a kid of minimal consciousness who never fully awoke, who dreams it still. Then comes a time—call it early autumn, all too close upon the long, hot, thunderstormy summer—when the stream slows down, pools in the shade of a big, old cottonwood just beginning to yellow, when it stills, green and glassy. Wide awake now, we look into its mirrored surface and name the reflection we see there. Some call it nostalgia; others call it the self in its slow shaping.

# THE MUSIC OF SILENCE

What I remember is standing alone in the empty, yellow-tiled first-floor hallway of Bond Hill Elementary School. It was 1942 and I was ten years old, and everyone else in my grade was in the twice-a-week music class taught by Mr. Alfred Hartzell (whom we called A. H. because for us, there in the midst of the Second World War, to which our uncles and the fathers of our friends had been called away to fight for the preservation of democracy, A. H. stood for Adolf Hitler). I was standing out there feeling a mixture of agony and relief. I knew that I was in disgrace with fortune and men's eyes—or at least children's—but all the same, if anyone had come by and asked me, I would have gladly informed them (even though, being a kid, I couldn't have explained why) that I would far rather have been out there than in that class.

From just outside the classroom door I could hear them singing. As usual, they were wallowing through the heavy seas of one of A. H.'s many "medleys," the sequences of old favorites—his—that he regularly forced our class to set sail upon: "Suwannee," "My Old Kentucky Home," and "Camptown Races," which was what I thought I could hear my classmates struggling along on just then in two-part harmony. At least they weren't having to struggle with overcoming my discordances.

Fifteen minutes or so earlier, in the midst of our singing "My Old Kentucky Home," in which I was participating as obliviously as I participated in everything else in my early

education, Mr. Hartzell had suddenly brought the whole class
to a halt with a sharp rapping of his baton on his desktop. He
was a small, dark, thin man, with thin black hair to match and
a little mustache. Maybe he *was* Adolf Hitler. Standing erect
in front of us—we, at his command, were also standing—he
said, "I smell a rat." He wiggled his mousy little nose above
his black toothbrush mustache and sniffed. He said, "Let's find
out who the rat is."

He made his way through the class, listening to us one by
one. Each of us sang a few bars, solo, a cappella. "Can't you
hear the darkies singing. . . ." He nodded, went on to the next.
He had started at the back of the room, so I, waiting my turn
near the front as obliviously as ever, was one of the last. When
my turn came, ever the good student, I leaped to the challenge
with alacrity, a young slugger just waiting to crunch that first-
pitch fastball. But it was past me before I got the bat off my
shoulder. Like the ump from hell, A. H. was waving me out of
the box, pointing toward the door.

"You," he said. "Get out."

So, having whiffed in my big turn at bat, I was both relieved at being removed from the scorn of my teammates and
shamed at having been identified as the contaminant in their
midst: the rat, the cracked vessel through which their liquid
tones spilled out, the incompetent my father would soon des-
ignate me (plastering that label on with the Super Glue one
ends up picking forever at the scabs of). But standing alone in
that empty, yellow hall, listening to my classmates making a
joyous if muffled sound on the other side of the door and ignorant of whether I would ever again be admitted into their
chorus, I was not thinking about what they might be thinking
about me. I was thinking instead about what I'd say if someone came down the hallway and asked me what I was doing
standing out there during class time: the principal, perhaps,
or Mrs. Norcross, my first-grade teacher, whom I adored

the way we all adore forevermore our first-grade teachers. Should I answer with what I felt? Hitler hates me. Or should I take it like a man? I can't carry a tune.

■

The fact is, I simply *cannot* carry a tune. This is unfortunate, I suppose, in that I can *hear* all those tunes—from Bach to Jerome Kern to the songs of my own operatic collaborator, Eric Stokes—perfectly well in my head (or so I think, anyway). I just can't reproduce them externally, not with a hum, not with a whistle, not with the appropriate vocalizations. It leaves me standing and mouthing the alma mater at graduation and "The Star Spangled Banner" at baseball games and those wonderful hymns on my rare forays into churches while all around me everyone else is letting loose with melodious gusto. Unfortunate, yes, but not, I think, a crime against humanity. A minor disability, no doubt—like a limp or a liver spot, the sort of thing people can't help taking notice of—but not, I believe, a reason to be banished from the society of one's fellows, pointed out as a barbarian who has somehow infiltrated and must be driven back outside the walls, back into the outer darkness among the savage and uncivilized, lest he contaminate the decent people. But even out here—and now, where, being a slow learner, I find that the years have sharpened rather than dulled my senses—I know all too well the smell in the smoke that drifts out above the great choral masterpieces on which he gently laid the needle down every evening after work.

Adolf, it *was* you after all!

I, too, can "hear the darkies singing," but I do not think they sing for you.

Nor is it, needless to say, a tune I can (or would) carry myself, though in my mind—where I hear things ever so clearly—it resonates well enough. I remember a couple of black kids at Bond Hill Elementary School—both from the same family, as best I can recall, though neither in my grade— and I wonder now, as it never would have occurred to me to wonder back then, how they managed to stoop to the labor of those medleys and wrap their voices around the rancid senti- mentalizing of "Old Black Joe" without ending up out there in the hall with me. Or *were* we all out there in the same hall together, only at different times, staring at the same yellow walls, smelling the same bitter smell, not knowing—how could we? we were just kids—what we'd say if someone came along and asked what we were doing out there?

My banishment wasn't permanent; no doubt even the A. H.'s of the world have to compromise their principles at times. But when I was readmitted to the class the next time it met, and for the remainder of the school year—of my entire elementary school education, in fact—I was ordered in no uncertain terms, thereby setting the pattern for the rest of my musical life, not to sing. I was to stand up, sheet music in hand, with all my classmates, who so far as I could tell held none of this against me and no doubt relished the entertainment value of the whole scenario. I was to open my mouth and move my lips, but not one of the beautiful notes I heard ringing so clearly inside my head was to escape me. Not a drop of my lemon juice was to be allowed to sour the sweet, white milk of Mr. Hartzell's medley.

So it was that I learned, as the man says, silence and exile— though not (being, as I said, a slow learner) cunning. I never was very good at cunning, and by the time I figured out what it was, I had also figured out that it wasn't something I really wanted to practice. But by then, silence and exile—the latter, of course, primarily an interior kind, the feel if not the fact of it—were my well-established modes, because in the best of pedagogical traditions (as if my parents had been taking instruction from the most expert of educators), what I learned at school was being soundly if silently (of course) reinforced at home. There was, in fact, a lot of cunning going on there as well, but there was no way I could learn that because it was, well, so cunningly managed that I didn't even know it was there.

It's easy enough to con a kid, but a conned kid with any brains at all eventually figures out he's being conned even when he doesn't know what the con is all about. And though I mostly wandered through childhood as oblivious as a dog to the intricacies of the social life surrounding me, content that there was a spot of sunshine to lie in and that my bowl was being filled regularly, I wasn't a total nitwit. Something *was* going on. Nobody would talk about it, of course. My questions all went unanswered or were cut off abruptly with, "Nobody cares about that sort of stuff." Be quiet, was the message; get out of here with your discordances.

I got the message, and I got out. Silence: look how well I learned it; even now, here, I haven't yet uttered a single note of what it was all about. I learned my lesson as well as any Hollywood gangster living up to his professional code of honor: Don't be a stool pigeon. Don't sing.

The only thing I sensed was that under the solid weight of all that silence (like a body encased in concrete and dumped into the river) lay a secret, and given the kind of questions I had already given up asking—questions about the family—it had to be a secret about family. Moreover, given how insistently it was pointed out that my questions about family weren't fitting, it had to be a secret about how I fit into that family, and if there was some question about that, then obviously I didn't fit into that family quite the way I should have. And if I didn't fit, then obviously I didn't belong. I was an exile.

Worse yet, every question I asked proved once again that I

was the sour note threatening to curdle the warm milk of familial comfort from which I, too, took nourishment. So I fell silent and took my accustomed place just outside the door, where I could tune in on the soft melodies of family life humming pleasantly away inside. But there was also the smell of smoke wafting out now and then—just my father's cigars, perhaps, but as we know, where's there's smoke . . . Maybe it's true that the suppression of one sense sharpens another. Maybe when in there one just gets accustomed to the odors that shock one out here. I can't honestly say that even in those circumstances I preferred being out here—in all probability I longed to be in there with the rest of them, which looked like a pretty good place to be—but out here, silenced, exiled, I lifted my nose to the familial air and sniffed out . . . something.

There is, people often tell me, always something. That's a paranoid prescription I couldn't possibly live by, but there was, in this case, something: there was, in fact, a body solidly encased in all that concrete silence.

■

That's another story, but see how well I've learned. Even now, babbling away here, I can still stay true to the silence in the midst of language, still take up my well-learned (well-taught) position just outside the door of tell-all sociability—perhaps not without, this time, a touch of cunning. Having learned silence, the next step might be learning how and when to use it. Having accepted exile, the next step might be learning how to negotiate the border between "in there" and "out here." Having learned those things, perhaps cunning is the natural, the unavoidable, concomitant. And if I've reached that point, who knows, in time I may even learn to sing (maybe a little, by myself, in the shower). There are amazing melodies taking wing in my head at this very moment.

And there are always those who don't want to hear them.

That—not the particular tune I'll try to trill another time—is my purpose here. Remember that kid standing all by his lonesome in the yellow halls of Bond Hill Elementary School, banished from polite society for his crow's croak of a voice? Many years later he sat, stiff and inarticulate as a board, in the recital hall of the Walnut Hills High School Music Department. It was the last month of his senior year, and there was one graduation requirement that—despite his straight-A average—he still had to fulfill: the music requirement, of course, which he had steadfastly managed to avoid all those years, and which could now be completed only by passing a singing test. A singing test! To graduate from high school! He'd already been accepted at a prestigious eastern university, but now he seemed likely to languish in the twelfth grade instead, unable to satisfy that one final graduation requirement, exiled forever from the glamour and opportunities of higher education, serving the life sentence of silence and solitude he'd long since sadly accepted.

This time he was not up front but cowering in the very center of the auditorium, huddled among friends who had also postponed fulfilling this requirement (though out of laziness or indifference, not fear) and who would soon warble their way happily along toward the commencement platform, which he figured he'd be watching from the audience, delighted for them but banned from the ceremony himself.

*This* music teacher, however, was no Hitler, though she might have been one of his officers, just holding her nose and doing her job. He doesn't remember her name, but she knew his: she had a list! And, of course, she found him there, in spite of the protective coloration of friendship that concealed him. If there was one thing he'd begun to learn, both from his own experience and elsewhere, it was that they always find you, wherever you are. They have lists.

She called out his name, looking around the hall for him

from up front, beside her piano. She couldn't recognize him, never having seen him around the Music Department, but there was no escape. He stood slowly, the huge lump in his throat the product in great part of his knowledge that trying to wrap his vocal cords around a single note of the song he was being asked to sing—"America the Beautiful"—would be like trying to swallow a baseball. But when Mrs. What's-her-name struck a note on the piano—I couldn't tell you which—inescapably, he "sang": "Oh byoo-ti-ful . . ."

And she said, "Thank you, that's quite enough."

And it was. A few weeks later, standing onstage on a riser in the big auditorium during graduation ceremonies, he spotted her out there in the audience, sitting right in front of his parents, and she—could it be?—winked at him. Maybe she just blinked, or maybe she was one of those people who always tears up at public occasions—weddings and funerals and the like—he couldn't be sure. His eyesight, sad to say, wasn't all that much better than his musical ability, though when his girlfriend, one tier down and several people over to the right, turned her head and winked at him, he saw that clearly enough, and everything else went quite out of his mind. For just a moment there, thanks to those two women, the smoke cleared, and he felt a sudden, unexpected absence of exile. Barbarian that he was, he stood, briefly and tentatively to be sure, among the decent, civilized folk, fully aware that he didn't really belong. Still, he would, if he could, burst into song, speak foreign languages fluently—even English. The briefest glimpse of an occasion such as this was enough to attune his heretofore unmusical mind to arpeggios of possibility.

If only his nose weren't so sensitive.

# PREMATURE BURIAL

## 1. FINAL EXAM

On my nineteenth birthday, early in May near the end of my first year away at college, I received a card signed, "Love, Aunt Jean & [in a different handwriting] Aunt Rose." All the other cards that came, the usual ones from my parents, my grand-parents, my father's brother and sister, I glanced at and then (although this might seem a touch callous, it was, after all, the eve of final exams) casually disposed of. This one, however, I kept. It was a puzzler.

I had to admit, as I laid that card aside for the time being, that I was a poor student when it came to family taxonomy. I had accepted by that time the embarrassment of being intro-duced and reintroduced to the same people on something like an annual basis at weddings and funerals and various holiday events, to say nothing of chance meetings at my grandparents' apartment or Aunt Ethyl's home. For the most part, I had managed to master the art of faking it, generally at least rec-ognizing the name if never quite clear on the connection. Doing a lot of nodding and mumbling. My father's mother's side seemed always the most complex, almost indecipherable in its variously named branchings, though over the years some of those names finally took up permanent residence on that mental taxonomic chart. My father's father's relatives were, so far as I knew then, nonexistent. My mother's family, on the other hand, was small, unforgettably bizarre, and, for reasons I couldn't possibly have known at the time, showed so little interest in me that, though I certainly couldn't forget them, I felt no particular obligation to remember them, either.

These two aunts, however, Jean and Rose, I was quite sure I had never heard of.

But it was, as I said, finals time, I had other matters of importance on my mind—English, and physics, which I was on the verge of failing, and homesickness, and my obnoxious roommate, for example—and so I rather quickly let them slip from my mind. Not their birthday card, however. When it came time to pack for home, I tossed it into the bottom of my suitcase. I'll ask my mother when I get back, I told myself. She'll clear up this little mystery easily enough, and then I'll be just that much less stupid about who's who in the family.

## 2. FISSURES

The world is full of fissures, vast man- and woman-holes into which people suddenly disappear, sometimes with a little shove from those close by. And afterward, no one says a word.

For some years while I was in elementary school—the exact dates, if I ever knew them, elude me now—we had a boarder who lived in our third bedroom, the one opposite the bathroom at the top of the stairs and to the right, just before you crossed the short hallway to my parents' room on the left and the room my brother and I shared on the right, with its bunk beds, its nautically patterned linoleum rug (all white ropes and blue anchors), and its view of the backyard with the lone, enormous willow tree. The boarder's name was Ruby, the only name I knew her by, and I remember her as being tall, though perhaps that was only in relation to my mother (stepmother actually, though I didn't know it yet), who wasn't, and as having dark, wavy hair—what I think was called marcelled (though, of course, I didn't know that at the time either)—bright-red lipstick laid on thick as plaster, and pale, lustrous cheeks.

If she had a life outside that bedroom, I wasn't aware of it. She must have had a job, though, to pay the rent, and must have come and gone like any normal person, and used the bathroom and taken some of her meals at the kitchen table, but I have no recollection of seeing her around the house, of having any meals with her or meeting her coming into or out of our one bathroom. And, of course, I never saw her in her own room, where the door was always tightly—inviolably—shut, whether she was there or not, a fact that leaves me wondering as I write this how it is that I have such a clear image of her.

She must have been a very private person.

She lived with us, it seems to me, almost as if she were already gone. Or maybe—what would I know? I was just a kid—we allowed her to live with us as if we had already dismissed her from our lives.

I'm not at all certain what she was doing boarding with us; my parents apparently didn't feel they had any obligation to explain her presence to us children. I didn't know any other kids whose families rented out rooms, so there was no one else to compare this business of having a boarder with. I assume it must have had something to do with money—the small extra income that having a boarder could bring in—and Ruby was clearly an ideal boarder, so inconspicuous as to be barely a presence in the household. But it was never at all evident to me, even in retrospect, that her financial contribution was needed. Those were the waning years of the Great Depression, and my father, at least, had seen in his own parents' experience some of the destruction it had wrought, but he was becoming a reasonably successful businessman then, co-owner of an enterprise that was becoming more prosperous by the year;

his wife lived the life of the middle-class homemaker as pic-tured in the glossy magazine ads of the time for kitchen ap-pliances and floor waxes and Jello; his family lived in a fine, little, stuccoed two-story Tudor in a fine, little, suburban middle-class neighborhood. It still stands, in fact, looking just as fine as ever (rather finer, in fact, with fresh paint and the ad-dition of some flower beds), though we, quite inexplicably—they still weren't explaining things to us kids—left it at the end of my sixth grade year for the cramped two-bedroom quarters of a lower duplex on a street lined with identical ugly brick duplexes on small, treeless lots.

I wonder now where Ruby, if she was still living with us at that time, went when we moved into a place that seems to have reflected harder times (but in those more prosperous war years?) and had no spare bedroom. Likely she moved on well before that, though, and to a better situation, perhaps her own apartment; women were much in demand in the job market in those days.

This woman who lived alone even in the midst of others; this woman who lived inexplicably among us and then disap-peared from our life as inexplicably (to me at least) as she entered, never to appear again; this woman for whom no ex-planations will ever be forthcoming now that those who might have done the explaining are long gone (nor, given the familial penchant for lengthy silences, do I think they would be willing to explain even if they were still here to do the ex-plaining): she reappears to me vividly now as an emblem of absence, an icon of those whose lives are as opaque to the rest of us as other peoples' marriages, as distant from and yet as densely a part of the world we daily walk through as the molten core of the earth, whose very existence is at the same time both undeniably real—I can still see the mahogany waves of her hair, the crimson flash of her full lips, her cheeks pale and glossy as polished marble—and strangely irreal.

## 3. CRYPTOZOOLOGY

In some recent, random reading, I came across the term *crypto-zoology,* defined as the study of hidden life forms. I can't remember the context in which I found it, a book review perhaps, or the particular subject it was applied to there—microbial life, it might have been—but I liked both the term and its definition, in particular how wide-ranging it could be. The way I saw it, it could apply to anything from *E. coli* to extraterrestrial life. It didn't occur to me at the time that it could also be applied to half of my family.

To a small child, family is at once both the most known of worlds and a great cryptozoological mystery: outside the clear, bright space of the immediate household lies a tangled forest of connections, of complex interpersonal relationships, and, most mysterious of all, the strange behaviors of adults. No child would put it just that way, of course, but that doesn't mean that children aren't perceptive of the sway and balance and sometimes fall of the many varieties of apples on the family tree. The prudent child sits back and observes and bit by bit begins to put it together: who is related to whom and how and what their individual feelings are toward each other and how those feelings get managed and even, to some extent, what it means when adults do the strange things they do, such as disappearing into their workshops or spending hours on the phone or not listening to a thing you're saying. The more outgoing child just goes out and asks about these things, and therefore arrives somewhat more directly at pretty much the same level of understanding, with perhaps the exception of the oddities of adult behavior, depending on how gullible he or she is about the explanations adults give for the strange things they do.

But the most astute outgoing child, which I never was, would still have trouble penetrating a wall of silence, just as the most sensitive observer child, which I also never was—oblivious was more like it—might find some adult behaviors simply too cryptic to decipher. Even the most oblivious child, however, would sooner or later begin to take notice of certain things and, all other possibilities being unequal—too obvious that the adults would never explain, too risky to ask anyway—would eventually invent some sort of scenario that would enable him to rationalize, if not understand, the otherwise inexplicable drama of adult behavior.

So when my mother's sister and brothers took to doting on my younger brother, even I, lurking on the couch in the background with my book, a sullen outsider to all that gooey affection, could remain oblivious for only so long. I exempt Uncle Jule from this; he lived within his own fog of obliviousness and was never around long enough to bestow much affection on anyone, fifteen minutes per visit being about his limit before announcing that he'd "got to be moseying along." It was a long time before I understood where he was always moseying off to; for a young kid, the sex life of adults was as yet a total unknown. But when Aunt Mary, who worked at her brother Julius's drugstore, visited, or Uncle Ben descended from Chicago with his cranky brood for their annual summer visit, it was all too apparent whom the dim light of these generally glum people shone upon.

Did I want to be hugged and kissed or in any other way get caught in the sensory orbit of Aunt Mary when she walked in exuding a stomach-turning blend of each of the Coty cosmetics she'd been working with all day long at Uncle Jule's drugstore (where he himself specialized in outfitting grungy-looking old men with trusses)? Well, no, not really. Did I want to go for a ride with Uncle Ben in one of those odd automobiles he always arrived in, some ugly, bargain-priced new model that Nash or Hudson was trying to unload (he'd have been the ideal buyer for an Edsel if he'd lived long enough)?

Certainly not. Did I, on the other hand, long for the kind of attention they were bestowing on my little brother? Well, let's say I rationalized it, because he was, to put it quite simply— and I heard plenty of people simply put it this way—one of the most beautiful children who ever walked this earth. (And is, for that matter, still quite a handsome man, though the pure complexion and wide-eyed innocence and long, blond ringlets are all long since gone.) Who wouldn't shower all their love and affection on such stunning beauty? Strangers in the grocery store did it. There wasn't anything cryptic about it. I wasn't a total idiot. It wasn't that hard to figure out.

Of course, I understood it; it just so happened that I was wrong.

## 4. A KNOCK AT THE DOOR

It's no great news that every family has its secrets. And if they're not today's secrets, they're yesterday's, or the distant past's. Who were the adoptee's biological parents? On what shady business practices was the family fortune founded? Will the children ever be admitted to the real reasons for their parents' divorce? Why did she suddenly move out of town, he join the army? What's that cry we hear from the attic? Why that large bequest to a stranger in the will? Why the hush every time a certain person enters the room? Were they really Nazi sympathizers—or Communists, or Freemasons—or was that just a neighborhood rumor? How was the old homestead lost? How did you and Mom *really* meet? And what about those old crypto-Jews whose families changed their names and converted to Catholicism way back during the Inquisition but who carry on with an odd custom or two that no one understands the meaning of?

People die, fall silent or sullen or victim to blackmail or intimidation, go mad or to jail. Forgetfulness is endemic in some families, a genetic trait, and before long there's nothing left to forget. The map to the buried treasure is lost, the landmarks overgrown. The world itself seems to conspire. It's beyond coincidence how often the courthouse burns, all the records gone up in smoke. How frequently the crucial entries are missing from the family Bible, how there's a gap in the tape, a crash in the mental mainframe—"File Not Found!"— a gaping hole in the center of the family room large enough for a body to fall through, fresh cement in the cellar floor.

It's an old story.

Then—out of the blue, as they like to say, little thinking of all the connotations of that color—there's a knock at the door. "You probably wouldn't recognize me, but . . . " A strange voice on the phone, rising and falling in quavers of anxiety (long distance indeed). A letter from a lawyer in a far-off city. An unexpected birthday card.

Aunt Jean. Aunt Rose.

## 5. THE LITERARY LIFE, MISCONCEIVED

Mistaken identity is, of course, one of literature's great, perennial devices. As Saint-Savin the sophisticate explains to the naive Roberto in Umberto Eco's *Island of the Day Before:*

> A romance must always have at its base a misconception—of a person, action, place, time, circumstance—and from that fundamental misconception episodic misconceptions must arise, developments, digressions, and finally unexpected and pleasant recognitions. By misconception I mean things like a living person's reported death, or one person's being killed in place of another, or a misconception of quantity, as when a woman believes her lover dead and marries another, or of quality, when it is the judge-

ment of the senses that errs, when someone who appears dead is then buried, while actually he is under the influence of a sleeping potion; or else a misconception of relation.

Ah, those misconceptions of relation. Those "developments, digressions, and finally unexpected . . . [note the ellipsis here] recognitions." To say nothing of "someone who appears dead [and] is then buried, while actually . . .": poor Poe's worst nightmare (as defined in "The Premature Burial") of "certain themes of which the interest is all-absorbing, but which are too entirely horrible for the purposes of legitimate fiction," among which to "be buried alive is, beyond question, the most terrific of these extremes which has ever fallen to the lot of mere mortality," a subject "the mere romanticist must eschew." No "mere romanticist" he.

Mere mistaken identity, of course (as opposed to the tragic consequences of "a living person's reported death" or "someone who appears dead . . . while actually . . . under the influence of a sleeping potion"), generally plays itself out in literature as comedy *(Twelfth Night,* say, rather than *Romeo and Juliet),* though it can also have its darker side *(Great Expectations).* But on the whole, once the confusions of who's who are cleared up, everyone is satisfied—no, more: delighted *(Joseph Andrews)*—and all's well that ends well.

Ah, literature.


## 6. UNPACKING

So there we were, my mother and I, on a lovely, warm spring day, standing side by side in my bedroom in our new house that had, oddly, been completed just in time for me to move out of it and off to college. Was that mere coincidence, or should that have told me something, too? Well, as usual, obliviousness and rationalization—of my father's obsession with watching his very own house rise from the ground up, with, as he kept emphasizing, two-foot-thick foundations, factory foundations, foundations, it was implied, that nothing could ever shatter—locked hands across the path to such questions so tightly it never occurred to me to try to get through.

So there we were, on a weekday, workaday late-spring morning, just returned home from the suburban train station where she'd picked me up after my overnight journey back from the East Coast. This was romance, wasn't it? Train travel! Overnight in a Pullman car, tucked into an upper berth, peering out the window at the towns flashing by! My first year at college just ended! The Ivy League even! But let's not make too much of that; life among the prep-school boys had felt all too much like Poe's dreaded fate of premature interment. Foolish as ever, naive as ever, I was, at that particular moment, very glad to be home.

How does that famous line go? "Whom the gods intend to destroy they first" . . . what? Make happy? Blind?

It was the most ordinary of moments: my brother at school, my father at work, my mother standing beside me chatting, me tossing the dirty socks and shirts and underwear I'd brought home into the laundry pile on the floor, working my way down, finally, to the bottom of my suitcase.

"Oh yeah, I got this birthday card. Who's Aunt Jean? Aunt Rose?"

## 7. THE LITERARY LIFE, LITERALLY

Although I've read a few from time to time, mostly at the urging of friends and to fill in the potholes of a few empty hours, I've never been much of a fan of mystery novels, in spite of the fact that I'm even in a couple of them, sort of. I make a brief, dismal, and purely nominal hometown appearance in Jim De-

Brosse's *Serpentine Wall* as "the midget porn king of Cincinnati," who, I'm relieved to say, is killed in an Ohio River boat explosion even before the action begins. I come off somewhat better as a New York City detective in my former student Fred Huebner's *Picture Postcard.* These are not exactly the fictional roles I would have auditioned for, if I'd been invited, but at least one claims the use of my name was purely coincidental and the other considers it honorific; I'll leave the reader to decide which is which.

What does intrigue me about the genre is neither its rectitude nor its romance. On the one hand, we know how the usual pitched battle between the forces of good and evil is going to turn out, regardless of the charm of the evildoers or our understanding of the devilish social and psychological forces that made them do it, regardless of the compromised integrity and troubled private life of the good guys; it's just a matter of how we get there. On the other, we also know that by the time we've completed the journey, the landscape is going to be strewn with the dead, the disgraced, and the downright demented; it won't be a pretty picture. Fiction that so readily and regularly lives up to our expectations may have its satisfactions—if, for example, smugness is what one finds satisfying—but an understanding of life's or literature's complex possibilities generally isn't among them. It doesn't do *Crime and Punishment* for us.

But what it can do is dig. And I believe in digging. I dug in the sand when my folks took me to the beach. I dug holes in the empty lot behind our house big enough for my whole neighborhood gang to hide in. I dug into my dinner like I was out to devour the world. I did what I could to make my little digs into parental politics until I was warned to lay off, much as I also was when I attempted to dig into the question of all the photographs missing from the family album. Yes, girls too, eventually; I knew there was something I needed to burrow for there. And, of course, I learned to dig into books, into whole libraries, for what I wanted to know. And like every writer, I suppose, I discovered at last—being, as I've said, a slow learner and blind to much of what was going on both around and within me—that there was some point to digging into my own life: not for myself (that would have been the dull, therapeutic mode), but for what could inform the work, which was far more interesting.

So digging, I think, was what intrigued me about mystery novels: the hard, gritty, dangerous, down-to-earth work of digging up the dirt, digging out the facts, dredging through the muck, yes, even digging up the past, digging up . . . the bodies. And nobody, to my way of thinking, did it better than Ross McDonald, because whatever got dug up (often literally) in his novels—people, maybe, or cars, things that shouldn't be down there—had something even stranger rotting away beneath it. And when that was brought to the surface, when the layers of earth that had buried it under six feet of silence for all those years were finally shoveled aside, deliberately or by accident, there was no telling what the results might be. And yet one had to go digging for it. That was what it was all about.

It wasn't till after I'd read several of McDonald's mysteries that I came across a bit of biographical information and learned that what he was really digging up was his own life. It wasn't till then that I was forced to admit to myself that what really intrigued me about them was my own life.


## 8. CONVENTIONS

I had always thought that the image of someone turning "pale as a ghost," "the blood draining from her visage," was a purely literary convention. It's not. I saw it for myself that morning. She opened the card I handed her and read the names I'd named. The blood drained from her face. She turned white as a sheet. She said, "Your father will have to talk to you about this."

Even as she headed for the telephone to call him, I was still too opaque to understand what was going on. You didn't call my father at work, not any more than someone from work would dare to call him at home. Especially not for something so trivial as a name or two on a birthday card. Aunts: what was the big deal? It was like calling the rabbi down from the altar while he was reading from the Torah to ask if he knew where you could get a good knish. It was like calling the Reds's starting pitcher off the mound to ask if he could get your little brother a ticket for tomorrow's game, calling the surgeon out of the operating room for a Band-Aid, calling the president out of the war room. . . .

When she came back to tell me he was on his way home, I understood.

Actually, I didn't understand at all, that is, I hadn't the slightest idea what this was really about. But I understood. I understood it had to be something momentous. I was standing in the middle of the living room by then. I don't know how I got there. I didn't know where my mother had gone. Into hiding, it now occurs to me. I walked over to the big picture window that looked down into the backyard. Everything was green. There was a great industry of squirrels and robins going on down there. My world, I realized, was about to change. These mysterious aunts, Jean and Rose, by inscribing their names on an innocuous card had lit the fuse that triggered an explosion that was about to bring everything down. We've all seen footage of buildings being imploded: a puff of smoke, a pause, then the whole structure crumbles in upon itself. All in a silence as profound as that of those aunts I'd never heard from or of before. Aunts, whom I didn't know. My father, whom I could now see I also didn't know. And myself: where, if anywhere, did I fit into this? Here goes the family, I

thought—my first moment of anything resembling lucid-
ity—and here I go, and then the whole house, the whole
world, the thick, green carpeting and the peacock-back chair
and the picture window full of bright spring light and birds
and squirrels, began to spin around me, my first, last, and only
ever attack of vertigo.

## 9. TALES FROM THE CRYPT

Every story I have ever told of family secrets—and this is only
one of them—has brought the spirit of a comparable tale fluttering out from deep in the familial mausoleum of my listener.
It's not just that we have a fascination with what lies hidden,
silenced, buried, but that those things speak to us with a
power that derives directly from their status: when they get
the choke hold of the grave off from around their throats, what
they have to gasp out is the most important story of their
lives—and often ours—-because it is the story untold, the
story that has not been allowed to be told.

No wonder the House of Usher cracks apart and comes
tumbling down when Madeline staggers forth from the
"donjon-keep" where she has been entombed in its depths. It's
not just the shock of her awakening from premature burial
that brings down the house; it's what her very presence has to
tell us. Poe's worst nightmare is our own: the power of what
lies hidden—especially of what, and who, we have forced into
hiding—to shatter the foundations of the house we have built
atop the graveyard. *Poltergeist,* for all its otherworldly Hollywood hokiness, tells much the same story. But it is also the
story we should have known all along, because it is the
story—the only story—that will permit us to understand
what is happening, that will help us, like Poe's narrator, to
make sense of the encrypted life we are caught up in.

## 10. REINTERMENT POSTSCRIPT

Well, okay then, here it is. I hate to see grown men and women storm out of a room in frustration when all they wanted were a few words to settle them down. It's a story, like I said, so I suppose it has to have an ending, though I guarantee you, you won't much like it—I don't much like it myself, but it's the only one I've got—and you may go away as dissatisfied as before, perhaps muttering this time instead of storming. Anyway:

He was home by the time the living room floor settled back into place and I could risk taking a step or two again without feeling like falling. He told me to get in the car so we could go for a drive and talk. What is this thing about cars? We had a perfectly good living room to sit and talk in, a living room I'd never even had a chance to use yet, with brand-new furniture in a practically brand-new house. On the way out, I felt like I should be waving good-bye to all of it.

We didn't go very far. We parked, somewhere, on some side street, like a pair of lovers, except it was broad daylight, mid-morning still, and to my continuing amazement there were tears running down the face of this man I'd never seen cry before, this man I didn't know could cry, this man who'd long since shamed the "crybaby" out of me. Clearly, the world as I knew it was dissolving before my very eyes. Is this what the car was about: a container for this swamp of dissolution so that afterward we could paddle back to shore and leave it behind and settle back down on dry land as if we'd never taken this messy journey? He hoped so, I imagine, even as he unfolded the story of his first wife, my mother (my mother!), dying as a result of a childbirth infection, of his in-laws' brutal demand that he observe Orthodox custom by marrying the oldest (and totally unacceptable to him) unmarried sister, of the need he therefore felt to separate himself completely from that whole family, to bar them forever from access to me, to enlist the aid of his entire community, in fact, in burying them—yes, in burying *her*—so deep in the darkness beneath the solid, packed-down, sodded-over ground of his necessity, under such a grim weight of earthen silence, that there was no chance they would ever return to haunt him (or me) again.

Then he drove me home and went back to work, and the subject was never mentioned again. And, of course, I never made any attempt to contact Jean and Rose because if you are at sea in a small boat that has almost been swamped by a great wave surging over it out of nowhere—rogue waves, I understand they're called, that do not follow the rules you think are set for them but rise up from the morbid depths when least expected—you do not rush to the bow and challenge the ocean to hit you with another one; no, you cling for your very life to the wheel and your crew, survivors all, hushed by the magnitude of the power that's just rolled over them, no one even daring to mention the gurgle of the newly sprung leak below decks, an oceanic wall of silence rising up around them.

End of story.

Almost.

□

# HERB

*A Memoir*

You probably didn't know my father, and there's really no reason you should have, except that if you did, you probably would have liked him. Almost everyone did. And why not? There was a bigger-than-life quality to him, and not just from a kid's short perspective either. He was tall and well built and strikingly handsome, and with his neat mustache and shiny, brushed-back black hair, he cut such a dashing figure as a single young man in Cincinnati that they used to call him, after the movie idol of his time, of course, "the Sheik."

Or so he often told me. Because he didn't dash when I knew him. I never even saw him run, though I had enough trouble as it was as a kid keeping up with his long-legged stride. He was certainly a good-looking man, that much I knew, and he always dressed nicely, if conservatively, but there was nothing of the adventurer about him, nothing of the romantic. There was no smoldering gaze in his dark eyes. He rarely even danced with his wife. He didn't drink. I never heard him swear. If he was the model of anything, it wasn't passion, it was poise. He left for work every morning dressed in a dark suit and a clean white shirt, at exactly eight o'clock, after his single cup of Lipton's tea. He returned home at five, sat and read the newspaper, and let his eyes drift shut for a bit as he waited for his roast beef and mashed potatoes. Afterward, he made his daily phone call to his mother and then settled in for the evening to devour his latest *Reader's Digest* condensed book. Valentino, of course, was long since dead.

On Wednesday and Saturday nights he played gin rummy, in a silence broken only by the brief grunts that served equally to express frustration or delight, with a small group of male acquaintances, usually at one of their homes, while in another room the women played mah-jongg or canasta, chattering noisily all the while. Later in life, when I was a teenager and he finally felt prosperous enough to join a country club, he took up golf, though he never showed much enthusiasm for it. It was the only thing approaching physical activity—including yard work—that I ever knew him to do, though the lack of exercise never seemed to have any deleterious effect on his good health and his trim, solid physique. Neither did the Camels he puffed moderately for many years, the long, dark A. C. Tony cigars he later switched to and then gave up smoking for simply sucking on—before he gave up even those for candy, licorice being what he loved most. Except for one attack of hemorrhoids that required minor surgery, he was never sick. His hair, of course, slowly grayed over time, but otherwise it seemed that everything about him remained constant. Men's clothing styles changed slowly over the years, naturally, but his didn't.

He was in the wine business, co-owner of a bottling and distributing company with an older, wealthy German-Jewish bachelor partner with whom he had absolutely nothing else in common, but what it was exactly that he did at the office, we never knew. The only time I ever knew him to bring home news from work was the year he was elected president of the Ohio Winedealers' Association, a well-deserved if mostly honorary position that demonstrated the respect his peers in the business had for him. Otherwise, and to his credit I suppose, he didn't bring the office home with him, though many years later, when I worked for him, I came to sympathize with the frustrations he'd quietly faced as a businessman: wartime shortages, militant unionizers, cumbersome state and federal regulation of the alcoholic beverage industry, trucking and railroad strikes, plus the sharp and sometimes illegal activities of his big-time competitors. To this day, out of respect for him, I refuse to let a drop of Gallo pass my lips.

"Things always work out for the best" was one of his favorite maxims, but that, as I grew older, came to seem to me a rather strange article of faith for a man who'd seen his own parents lose everything in the stock market crash of 1929, who'd watched his first wife—Bess, my mother—suffer a slow and agonizingly painful death from complications and medical incompetence following childbirth, and who could surely not have been unaware of what went on in Nazi-dominated Europe between 1939 and 1945. And even faith itself came to seem strange to me for a man who never showed any signs of practicing the religion into which he'd been born beyond accompanying Zelda, his second wife and the mother who raised me, to temple on the High Holy Days. And even this was a task he happily relinquished to me as soon as he deemed me to be of an appropriate age. The only religious advice, if that's what it was, that I can recall ever receiving from him was to beware anti-Semites; they were, he assured me, everywhere, and they were out to get you. Unfortunately, he didn't tell me what to do about them.

But as that advice implies, he did have some strong opinions, regardless of how rarely they surfaced. He was a bit of a racist, of course, which appalled me as a youth—appalled me especially to discover how pervasive it was throughout the entire Jewish community—but didn't surprise me, since I rarely met anyone in that city who wasn't. And if he wasn't as vocal and vicious as most of the men in his crowd in their condemnation of the *schvartzes,* so many of whom were in fact the best or only customers of their businesses, his quieter slanders, when they came, expressed no less conviction. The poor of any race, of course, deserved their lot, which was purely the product of their own laziness and inexcusable in this, the land of opportunity and the greatest country in the world. Those who didn't like it here should go back where they came from. When asked, he would claim to be a Democrat—like most of his peers, his life and family and businesses had flourished under Roosevelt—but he always voted Republican.

The minor incident that epitomized for me the deep-set, unshakable foundations of his opinions occurred one day in my late teens when I was downtown with him, though what the particular occasion was—we didn't exactly pal around together—I don't remember. What I do remember is that we were walking south on Walnut, between Seventh and Sixth, when someone hollered at him from the sidewalk across the street. Over there I saw, pausing in the sunshine to face us, a man not unlike my father himself: tall, middle aged, nice looking, well dressed. He was waving and calling out, "Hi, Herb! How are you?"—ordinary, friendly stuff like that. But my father neither looked his way nor returned his greeting. He simply kept walking, that long-legged stride of his more determined than ever, and I had to scurry to catch up with him. When I did, and as we waited for the traffic light at Sixth, I asked him, puzzled as I was by his determination to ignore an apparently friendly greeting, who that man was. His answer, the only one I ever got from him, simply, "He's no good," was only more intriguing, of course. What terrible things had this otherwise friendly, decent-looking man done to get himself labeled "no good"?

I asked.

"Just no good," was the answer.

And that's all there was to it. There was no getting beneath or behind it. It was an opinion, I later came to understand, presented as a fact, an irrefutable fact, so fixed in his belief system that it required neither explanation nor defense, just as would happen in his declining years when we would be eating dinner together, he and I and perhaps my brother, at some pleasant restaurant, and he would pronounce his food, which was identical to what I had ordered and was presently enjoying, "terrible."

"You mean," I'd say to him patiently, "that you don't like it."

"No," he'd insist. "I mean it's terrible."

The world, for him, I can now see, was a wholly objective place; qualities resided solely in it, not in the perceiver. He was, without knowing it, as committed a materialist as had ever been encountered in the history of philosophy. His world was as solid as a brick, and you could knock your brains against it all you wanted, but you would only get a headache and a bruised forehead. No wonder he had neither patience nor sympathy for the opinions I brought to it, opinions about the Reds's chances for a pennant, about the potential of socialism, about the flavor of the steak we were sharing. If they didn't match the way he saw things, which was not a matter of opinion but pure, uncluttered, objective fact about the way things were—the Reds were losers, the capitalist free market was the only viable system, the steak was terrible—they simply weren't worth paying any attention to.

And when he was challenged by the Reds's dominance in the seventies? By evidence that capitalism was constantly being compromised by such socialist-tinged, anti–free market devices as price supports, government subsidies, and protective tariffs? By the sight of everyone else at the table drooling ecstatically over the sirloin? No problem. Nothing changed. Regardless of what strange notions others might have, for him the world itself was a stable place, and things still remained just the way they always were: perennial losers, the one true way, terrible. The argument from opinion, probably even the very potential for subjectivity, softened no bricks for him. He was at the reality dance, looking good in his midnight-blue tuxedo of absolute certainty, and he wasn't about to fox-trot to a different tune.

"Mac the Knife," he proclaimed, when he and the century were both in their sixties, was *his* song. He hummed it, turned up the volume when they played it on the car radio, and danced to it with the various women he dated after his second wife's death—a couple of whom he even married. One might wonder what Brecht and Weill would have thought of an aging, conservative businessman adopting this paean to their antihero as his theme song. He traveled widely then, too, as never before, and why not, having the leisure of retirement and the financial resources of a lifetime as a moderately successful entrepreneur. He joined a couple of the travel clubs popular at that time, which had their own planes and delighted their members with exciting new options every week and sometimes even surprise destinations, letting them know only the day before departure what kind of clothes to pack. He loved, I think, the safe, well-tended excitement of it: the assurance of comfortable journeys; traveling companions much like himself; decent food; safe, clean accommodations; and no problems—or, if there were problems, someone assigned to take care of them. Life was an adventure in certainty. He took cruises. He flew to Japan and India and Spain and Greece. He found that women of his age and social group were not quite so keen on world travel as he was and that things were pretty much the same wherever you went. The natives were dirty but friendly, and a Hilton was a Hilton. Given which, it was no great surprise that he ended up, finally, living in Miami.

There was a certain irony in that, however, and not just in the fact that by making that move, he did for a woman, his fourth and last wife, what he had always sworn he would never do for himself: retire to a place far removed from home and peopled by strangers. But perhaps it was for acts such as that that women as well as men liked him, as he did them. At the Orthodox Home for the Aged, where he spent his last years, the women residents practically cheered his arrival. And pleasing women, after his fashion, was something he'd had a lifelong devotion to; more than once I heard him say of some particularly troubled woman in his social circle that he both knew exactly what she needed to solve her problems and was quite capable of providing that solution himself, though so far as I'm aware he never did.

But Miami, Miami Beach in particular, had been the site of the disastrous financial calamity that had changed the lives and the fortunes of the family forever. It was there that his father—with no blessings from his mother, who like him had no desire to live among strangers far from home—had prospered with a resort hotel, and it was there that, along with the rest of the country, he, my grandfather, crashed in 1929. I have a wonderful photograph on my dresser, one that my brother, Skip, has lovingly had restored and copied for me, of a happy trio consisting of my father, the oldest; his brother, Ed; and their youngest sibling, Ethyl, posing in an obviously tropical setting, undoubtedly Miami Beach or its vicinity. Palm fronds hover above them; they are all in their early- to midtwenties; they are smiling; they are extraordinarily handsome people; they wear the clothing of the prosperous young of the Jazz Age, and it appears that they are dressed for the winter season: my father in an open-neck shirt and sweater, my uncle in a suit, my aunt wearing a bulky sweater coat. Though my father would, in 1928, be the first of them to marry, they all have the look of single people here, single people with youth, looks, cash, and flair: "free, white, and twenty-one," as they and their contemporaries used to say. Perhaps they are spending the holidays with their parents. The photograph is undated, but studying it through the magnifying

glass of time's resonance, I have a hard time not placing it in
the winter of 1927–1928. It's an especially poignant moment
for those of us who know, now, what lay just ahead of them.

Driven deep into debt—debt that my father worked many
years to help pay off, rather then letting them fall still further
into the disgrace of bankruptcy—the family was forced to return from Miami's sunny shores to the gray, wet winters and
humid, sweltering summers of the Ohio Valley: to whatever
low-paying jobs my grandfather, who had trained as an artist

and enjoyed his brief success as a hotelier, could find, and to the gloomy apartments where my grandmother held her family together with food and love and intermittent reminders of how much she had always hated Florida. Together, as many must have done during the depression, they fended off loss with family, all of them. My father found employment decent enough to match his sense of financial integrity and assumed his parents' debts. His siblings soon followed him into marriage. I followed Roosevelt's ascension to the Democratic nomination. Bess, my mother, didn't live to vote him into office. And once again my father's world came crashing down around him.

Brick by brick, I think, is how he must have begun to rebuild it after that, given how debilitated he must have been by loss and grief, but then, soon, with more and more strength and speed as he grasped what he was trying to accomplish, laying course upon course until he had finally walled it all off, that whole painful corner of his life, where no one need ever have access to it again. Including me.

A hard worker and a man of fixed intentions, that project took him less than a year. By then he was back in the world again, only this time it was a world of his own making: no longer a world of shifting tropical sand and fragile flesh and human error, however, but a world of brick-hard and unshakable certainties. A new world, his, made to his own specifications and in accord with another of his maxims: "If you want something done right, you have to do it yourself." And when he had done it, made it the way it had to be for him to live in it, he married again, that very next year, the gentle woman who provided him with a second son and became the only mother I really knew. And no one ever mentioned the wall, or what—and who—lay behind it.

Not for almost twenty years, at any rate, until in a moment of inattentiveness—the problem with constructing worlds of your own rather than living in the one we're all given is that they require constant maintenance—it developed a small crack, just wide enough to let the tiniest piece of information through. A slender envelope, a birthday card from relatives who weren't even supposed to exist, was all it was, though it might as well have been a letter bomb. I'd tell you how this discovery felt, but you can probably imagine, and, besides, this isn't about me, but about him. I could tell you, though, how my brother reacted when, at a mere fifteen, he was confronted by some malicious fool threatening to disrupt the family integrity by telling him that his brother—that is, me— wasn't his real brother: Skip decked the creep with one punch.

But the question with my father isn't what he did—that we already know—but: How did he do it? How, in a small ethnic community where everybody knew everybody else's business, past and present, did he manage, for nineteen years, to keep secret the very existence of someone from that one person who might most, of all people, have wanted—deserved—to know about her? Not why—I think we already understand that— but how?

You have to give him credit. It couldn't have been easy. It took commitment, dedication, thoroughness, an eye for detail, wide contacts and slick social skills, a clergyman's belief in his moral propriety, a politician's way with words, a con man's gift for manipulation, a lawyer's feel for just the right half truth ("Must have fallen out," he told me, whenever I asked about the photos missing from the family album), and, I suspect, an extortionist's sense of power. It took whatever it took to enforce a conspiracy of silence upon an entire community (with, of course, one small but growing exception). It took constant vigilance. It must have taken enough energy to have powered several thriving enterprises.

It took, finally, even after it was all over, long over, when it appeared that the wall had crumbled at last—for me, if not for him—an astounding sense of consistency. It took the belief that he had done something right and done it himself. It took the conviction that things always worked out for the best. It took an absolute belief in the concrete and immutable nature of the way things were and ought to be. It took just this man, with the mind and body, power and charisma, who might have accomplished anything, anything at all. It's not at all hard to picture him standing monumental as any father, his arms outstretched to ward off the relentless erosions of wind and sand and time, intoning, "I am Ozymandias. . . ."

You probably didn't know my father—and it's too late now, anyway: he died in 1983, just a year short of his eightieth birthday—but if you had known him, I'm sure you would have liked him. Everyone did. How could you not have liked a man willing to go to such lengths, a man possessed of such strength of character, such rock-solid convictions, such enduring qualities? I myself have a certain admiration for him.

☐

## THE DOG OF MEMORY

Why a man in his late sixties, happily ensconced in the great love of his later life, should be concerned with remembering his first kiss, I can't imagine, except that he's read several times lately in various versions of the popular press that one never forgets one's first kiss, and he's certain that the conventional wisdom, as always, must be onto something. He—well, okay, I—can't recall exactly where I read (or was it heard?) about the unforgettableness of the first kiss, but that's the least of my concerns. The fact is, I *have* forgotten it. The fact also is that given my present life, I shouldn't even *care* that I've forgotten it. Was it such a big deal, that first, unremembered kiss, so important that I should be letting the conventional wisdom get its cliché-stained hands around my wrinkling throat? Well, yes, you bet: that kiss was a long time coming— I wasn't exactly a kissable kid—and by no means an immediate prelude to subsequent smooching. It was a lonely lighthouse, that first kiss, on the romantically barren beach of my youth, a larger-than-life statue, like Rodin's (well, no, surely not at all like Rodin's) *Kiss.* And though it has not been a big deal for a very long time now—the big deal at this age being instead the state of memory itself—it is still with some dismay that I confess to not remembering it. No wonder I started out here trying to avoid looking foolish and ignorant by giving the problem to some anonymous third-person character.

Blame it on the creeping forgetfulness of age, time's relentless deterioration of mind and body, except that again the

conventional wisdom—this time with a fair amount of support from scientific research—tells us that's not the way it
works. It's recent, short-term memory that's the first to go,
rather than those fragments of the more distant past that have
long since taken up permanent residence in the tenements of
the brain, decrepit squatters upon whom ownership eventually
descends. I still remember the first telephone number we had
when I was a child (MElrose 5113), as well as a headlong dive
off a park swing when I was two or three, with my stepmother
and grandmother both looking on (or, more likely, not looking), as well as . . . well, you get the point. The beaches of my
mind—not unlike your own, I'm sure—are littered with the
detritus the tides of the past have swept up. And however
much you or I value those glittering bits of sea glass, no
beachcomber who ever passes that way is likely to find it interesting enough to bother to stop for a second look.

And somewhere back there, half or wholly buried in those
sands of time no doubt, washed over decade after decade by
the tides of forgetfulness, lies my first kiss. Well, no, not my
first kiss, of course, but the memory of my first kiss. Or rather,
*a* memory of my first kiss, which may or may not have much
to do with that first kiss itself or with the memory of it as it
resides in the mind of my co-kisser, assuming that she (who-
ever she is) is still alive (as indeed both I and the statistics on
male-female longevity would like to think she is). But where
is it? Since being informed that one never forgets one's first
kiss—no more than one forgets one's first-grade teacher (and I
remember Mrs. Norcross as clearly as I recall the burnt English muffin I just had for breakfast)—I have gone over the territory with the industriousness of one of those old men one
sees sweeping the beach with metal detectors in search of
other sorts of treasures and generally, I presume, with no more
luck than I've had. And though I've turned up quite a lot of
old stuff, some of it fairly interesting (never mind now) and

much of it no more identifiable than a rusted nail that yields no indication of what it was ever pounded into, that first kiss has yet to start my past detector clicking.

So what? you say. What difference does it make? And believe me, I'd be the first to join you in that shrug of indifference. What difference *could* it possibly make at this late date whether it was Gladys in the seventh grade or Diane in the eighth? But the fact is—blame it on the pressure of the conventional wisdom, blame it on age's desire to recapture youth, blame it on the current fad for nostalgia, blame it, if you want, on the weather, since it's in the peculiar climatic conditions of the past that, like Gulf storms swirling up the Mississippi Valley to drench the great North where I've lived most of my life, today's storms are often born—*I* care.

Not because of the kiss itself, which, given a bumbling adolescence that I generally do my best not to remember, I can't imagine having been especially romantic or even successful. (Did I hit her lips on target? Bump noses? Lock braces? For that matter, was I the kisser or the kissee?) No, surely not because of the kiss, which clearly didn't make much impact on my life (or I'd remember it as well as I remember the emergency appendectomy whose subsequent complications set me aside from most of my ten-year-old buddies for the better part of a year). Most definitely not because of the kiss, which in the history of kisses since was at best a first small drop of rain preceding the downpour—well, okay, the afternoon shower—to come, a damp peck on the cheek that serves at best to make one look up at the swollen skies. Who, indeed, could care about such a kiss?

Memory's, however, another matter, especially when the world is boxing your ears with its insistence.

*Speak, Memory,* orders the title of Nabokov's memoir, as if it were a dog that'd sit up and recite the past for a Milkbone or an ear scratch. But memory's a slyer mutt than that, not beyond perking up its ears, wagging its tail, and then nipping your fingers. And for a word of praise from its master it would just as soon dig up an imagined tale if it can't recall exactly where it buried that bone it thinks you're looking for.

■

When I was a college sophomore, someone—no, of course, I don't remember who—taught me a trick for remembering an almost limitless number of words, an old mnemonic device that (as best I can recall) worked something like this. For each number from one to ten (or was it zero to nine?), memorize a specific image: one was maybe oil, two was a table, three was a thimble, four a fountain, five a fish, six a sandwich, and so on. You get the alliterative point. And that's about all there was to it. You had your private basket of little hooks to carry with you wherever you went, just in case you were asked to hang a list of words up in the closet of your mind. Then, when someone gave you a word, you simply hooked it onto the pre-existing image or images to make a memorable picture. Instead of remembering *skunk* when you were given the first word in some interminable and insipid list, you visualized a skunk opening a can of 10W30. The weirder your mental image the better, the easier the recall. Needless to say, you didn't reveal that that was what you were doing; you just gave a look of intense concentration, as if this were the intellectual equivalent of cleaning the Augean stable. By the time you got up to, say, number thirty-five on the list, and the word was, say, *brother,* you were picturing your brother with a thimble (for three, remember?) on his finger trying to pick up a dead fish (for five, of course). Who could forget that? You could easily do a hundred or more words if your audience had a vocabulary that was up to it. (Abstract words were a little trickier, but given the nature of my audiences, that was rarely a problem.) You could recite the list as easily backward as forward, give out the words for numbers called at random or the number for a word selected at random. Women swooned. Men backed off in terror. It was a cheap parlor trick, but for a brief period in my life I loved it and would have gotten someone to shill for me at parties—"Hey, Al, show Sharon here that memory thing you do"—except that it was never necessary.

Funny, I haven't thought about that in twenty or thirty years. I'm surprised I still remember how it works—if, in fact, that *is* how it works.

There was a point to this, though.

Something about memory as a trained dog.

For entertainment purposes only.

The researchers of memory, those scientists who tweak the poor, befuddled brain to see how and where it stores its stuff and by what sly devices and with what dubious accuracy it struggles to retrieve what it can—what should we call them? memorists? memorialists?—have long confirmed the conventional wisdom. No, not about the first kiss, though that's something that in my humble opinion they might profitably do some interesting research on, but about the more general notion that certain significant moments—for example, one's first kiss—are embedded in one's memory forever, like fossils in limestone (or race forever around the maze of the brain's electric circuitry like a subway train with no conductor aboard and no scheduled stops). The electric moment is exactly what it is; the psychologists even have a name for it: flashbulb memories. Where were you when FDR announced the attack on Pearl Harbor? ("A day that will live in infamy," I heard from the backseat of the family Chevy on the way home from a Sunday visit to my grandparents.) When JFK was assassinated? (In the midst of conducting a student conference in the mildewy stench, which my rancid olfactory recall still exudes, of my basement office at the University of Kentucky.) King? Lennon? When Challenger exploded or Pan Am 103 went down over Lockerbie? When the secret of your birth was first revealed? When your spouse first confessed . . . ?

Well, some episodes are more personal than others, more traumatic, more, I'm sorry to say, memorable. And according to the professionals and the amateurs alike, a first kiss is supposed to be one of them.

Is there a difference, I wonder, between *memorable* and *unforgettable*? To put it at its tritest, is a memorable occasion the equivalent of an unforgettable face? (Remember that regular *Reader's Digest* article, "The Most Unforgettable Person I Ever Met"?) Or is there something subtly but significantly different here? Does the clear, direct, and audible—you can practically hum it—association of *memorable* with *memory* and *memorial* suggest itself as something so important that we would, if only we could, always choose to remember it, whereas the negative prefix of *unforgettable,* along with its antonymic root, implies that it's something that, were it possible, we'd be happier to forget? Do two negatives connote a dubious positive?

If my first kiss wasn't memorable, was it then forgettable? So utterly forgettable, so antonymically unrememberable, that I don't get to have access to a simple, inconsequential little thing like this that's apparently available to everyone else?

I whistle up the good dog memory.

"Fetch," I say.

She just sits and stares at me with those big, brown Labrador eyes.

Eventually she tires of this. She did want to earn her biscuit, though. So she goes off and roots around out of my sight for a bit, then comes back with . . . ah, no. Please, not that one. I thought we'd buried that one deeper than any dog could dig. But she lays it at my feet anyway, all crusted with dirt and soggy where she's had her mouth around it.

This is not entertaining.
"Okay," I say, "you still get your biscuit."
I'm a sucker for retrievers.

My high school yearbook was called *The Remembrancer,* a name
we took for granted at the time since that's what it had always
been called, but that strikes me now as a little silly, phony, ar-
tificial, an almost embarrassing, high schoolish (of course),
made-up word that, nonetheless, makes its point, even gram-
matically. Obviously it speaks in its semantic root to memory,
to remembering—that's what yearbooks are all about—but
that clumsy suffix, that stuttering -er at the end, gives it an
unexpectedly active role. It's not supposed to be a passive
thing, this oversized volume with the heavily textured blue
cover with its deeply incised gold title, its midcentury year,
and its classical seal (*"Sursum ad Summum,"* it advised us: Rise
to the Highest). It wasn't meant to just lie there any more
than we were, closed and unconsulted, gathering dust in the
back of the closet or some far corner of the attic, boxed up and
ignored. It's (as it expects us to be) a doer . . . er . . . er . . . er.
Grrr.

It nips at your ankles with all the usual things, of course:
individual photos of the faculty and senior class and class officers; group photos against an identical background, on the
steps to a side entrance, of all the homerooms from grade
seven to grade eleven; carefully posed "action" photos of sports
teams and thespians and newspaper editors; cutesy photos of
the Best Dancers dancing, the Best Dressers all dressed up, the
Most Popular and Mostly Likely to Succeed being popular and
successful. It wants to play, and the name of its game is, When
this you see, remember me. It's got its teeth into the toe end
of an old sock and wants you to tug at the ankle end. And I'd
love to, because somewhere in there—the Chess Club (not

likely; almost all male), Eastern Star (hardly; no Jews), the Modern Dance Society (not impossible), the Latin Club (hmmm)—is the object, the subject, the coparticipant, the forgotten her-of-my-first-kiss. But as soon as I pull back, it lets go, and I'm left holding the limp elastic of an empty sock with a hole in its toe, a book of glossy pages full of faces and names in which I can't find *the* face, *the* name.

The autographs and scrawled greetings, the senior year farewells—"Lots O Luck," "Good knowing you," "Your friend," or the obsequious "To a great guy!"—don't provide a clue. Even if she'd signed in—and who knows, maybe she did—what was she going to say, after all, knowing that others would be opening those pages to inscribe their names as well: "To a swell kisser"? Not likely. Not even if it were true.

It's beginning to seem that *in* the past there are no clues *to* the past, that it's only in the present, if anywhere, in some still active corner of today's brain or upon a chance tomorrow meeting at which she recalls, at first sight of me (but what are the odds that she'd even remember me, aged and changed, bearded and balding?), that it was her first kiss too (but was it?), that we can find what we need of the past.

■

"The past," as L. P. Hartley says so poignantly in "The Go-Between," "is another country." But they don't, as his story goes on to assert, "do things differently there." They don't *do* anything there. Whatever they did there, whatever we did there, is done. Finished, kaput, over. A buried bone. I can't go back and join the Art League, try out for the football team, or raise my GPA. I can't, I am happy to say (and I hear this sigh of relief from others with some frequency as well, especially when it comes to those junior high and high school years), go back there at all. It is the Oakland of our lives: there is, as Gertrude Stein might have said, no longer any there there.

And yet, of course, though we can no longer take up residence there, it inhabits us. It fills us, sometimes, like a populous city, its crowded street scenes and intimate interiors playing themselves passionately out on the strange inner screens of our minds, sometimes over and over again, and often whether we desire to sit through another showing or not. Disney never had such a captive audience, not even for the R-rated stuff. If we make our visits to that distant country, it's only, as Blake would have it, as mental travelers. There's no need for passport and visa, for airline and hotel reservations or visits to the currency exchange; we travel there on our own schedule, or we're suddenly, unexpectedly, transported there by some out-of-control inner travel agent. But in the land of the past we find we're spectators only, not participants. We're fluent in the language, but no one talks to us. They seem too preoccupied even to notice our presence, and they're not the least bit willing to take us on guided tours of the great monuments. I want to ask directions—"Can you tell me, please, how to get to the First Kiss?"—but my every effort is ignored as they go about doing exactly what they were doing on my last visit, what they've always done and always will be doing: acting (but it's no act) as if they don't understand a word of my strange language, though it has the same syntax, the same vocabulary, as theirs, rendering me (and in my very own past!) quite invisible.

It all feels like the snipe hunts of my childhood summer evenings, when we conned some younger kid into getting a bag and waiting quietly in the depths of the forest—a rather scraggly little woods, actually, though, of course, we needed to hype the danger level to make it into a test of bravery and endurance—while we drove the putative prey, the infamous snipe, in his or her direction for capture. So here I wait, the empty sack of my mind wide open and hungry for its catch, assuming that the good dog of memory is beating the bushes

< 57 >

on my behalf to flush the quick rabbit of that first kiss out of hiding and send it hopping into my clutches. But all the while, just as the rest of us used to return to a game of kick-the-can in someone's backyard while our poor victim hunkered down in the growing dark, afraid to stay and embarrassed to return, the old dog is snoozing on the living room carpet, a piece of polished shin bone lying beside her whitening muzzle and only the occasional twitching of her legs betraying any dream of the hunt. And I am still sitting in the dark, remembering nothing. Shamefaced, I have no choice but to leave that darkening forest, where vision grows more and more dim, and return to the lighted present.

So is there any sense asking *Where was I?* when it seems that the only valid question is *Where am I?* As Archimedes longed for the fulcrum that would enable him to weigh the world, the present is perhaps the only point of balance from which we can pry up the past and understand just how it weighs upon us. Or should we say, how it lifts us up *(Sursum ad Summum!)* on the other end of the seesaw of our lives? We are dogged throughout our lives by memories—the good, the bad, and the indifferent—but they're not our past, those memories, but with us in the here and now; memories, unlike the remembered events, are not what we were but part of all we currently are. That first kiss: *c'est moi*—or so the memory of it would be, if only I could find it.

But, of course, as every aging body can tell you (proving yet another piece of conventional wisdom: that time will tell), I am not what I was. And maybe that's what's so important for us about memory: what time deconstructs, memory attempts to reassemble. It's no parlor game after all; it's our very lives. Willed forgetfulness, the deliberate disremembering of pain or trauma, is surely understandable—who wants to suffer that again, even in thought?—but at the same time, it's a hacking off of a significant chunk of who we are, a severing of flesh and bone, and generally no matter how hard we try, that phantom limb of the past still aches from time to time. It reasserts itself in the where we are, and not always with discomfort, either. Just as often, I'd say—more often, I'd hope—it throbs with the joy of old loves no longer physically at our side; with the elegant ease of events long past being folded into the fabric of our lives, like the long fly ball of my youth arcing down into deep left field out of the glare of the lights to settle comfortingly into my outstretched glove; with the solace of an old dog laying her heavy head in our lap, reminding us that she's always there whenever we want to play fetch, though there may be times when weariness or preoccupation or just plain forgetfulness prevents her from bringing back the exact bone we sent her off for.

# REMEMBER THE ALAMO

And it is also true that music heard in the past can make the whole machinery come to a halt and dumbfound the world for a moment.

—Clarice Lispector, *The Apple in the Dark*

Not two months after being told that I have an ancestor who died here, I am standing in the Alamo, trying to look like just another tourist but reading these bronze plaques labeled "Heroes of the Alamo" as if they hold the clue to my very existence. It takes me a while to realize that these plaques, which are mounted on the inside walls of the old mission church of San Antonio, are in alphabetical order. Trying to get away from behind the crowds of schoolkids and military people from the local army and air force bases, I have moved to the rear of the building and started with the list of names beginning with *M* and *N,* so I find myself having to work my way all the away around, past Travis and Bonham and Bowie and Crockett until I come to the right plaque. "Robert Fishbaugh," it says, identifying his home state as Ohio. The book on the history of the Alamo that I will soon pick up in the so-called museum—as famous historical sites go, this one is, to be frank, a little on the seedy side—will identify Robert Fishbaugh as coming from Texas. Just like him, I think.

On the paternal side of my family, they didn't arrive in this country until the 1880s, and no one got to Texas till my cousin when her husband was stationed at Lackland Air Force Base briefly in the mid-fifties. On the maternal side, however, *which we do not talk about,* it appears we were in America at least a half century earlier—give us well over a century in Texas, then—in the person of a veritable Texan (or Texian, as it says around here) hero, one of those 192 foolhardy volunteers who chose to step across Colonel Travis's imaginary line (only one man had the good sense not to) on, as the tour guide rhythmically pounding out his memorized speech over a crowd of blue-uniformed men and women behind me says, "that fateful day in February of 1836." Just think: what if it had been my great-great-great-grandfather himself who had decided that he wanted to leave Cincinnati and participate in the opening of the West, instead of (as best I can figure out from the minimal and dubious information the family has been able to provide me with) his older brother, this Robert Fishbaugh? Or Fishblum. Or Fishman, which is the name I finally came to know the family by, though the evidence seems to indicate that they produced name changes as rapidly as offspring in the New World. And "Robert"? Could he really have been named Robert? Abe or Hyman or Izzie, very possibly. But "Robert Fishbaugh"? Just like him, I think.

Mostly what I want to know is: What was he doing there? Here.

Because I am sitting here in the garden behind this mid-eighteenth-century Spanish colonial mission, sitting on a stone bench under a spreading live oak tree, with a cactus garden in front of me and a pair of enormous palms looming behind me, sitting here all alone in the warm, winter, early-afternoon sunshine of the late twentieth century, wondering what I am doing here myself. Oh, I can explain what I'm doing in Texas readily enough: the usual academic bit, escorting a student group on a January-term off-campus outing. But what am I doing *here*?

My students have made their quick pass by the Alamo and, alert as ever to the historical stupidities of their country, seen it quickly for what it is: a minor monument to imperialism and machismo. ("I shall never surrender or retreat," says Travis in his last letter, an appeal for reinforcements against Santa Anna's thousands.) Now they are down there along the River Walk somewhere, trying on handwoven cotton shirts and dresses from Mexico or sipping strawberry daiquiris at a riverside café and watching the tourist boats glide by. But I am thinking of it as the final resting place (even though I read in this thin, little book I've just spent $6.95 on that they still don't know where the mass burial site is) of a Fishbaugh. Or Fishblum. Or Fishman. One of those people, anyway. My mother's family. Not a single one of whom, until just recently, I had ever met in person.

■

Less than two months before this, just a couple of days after Thanksgiving, I was sitting in a franchised shopping mall restaurant, one of the nicer kind with tablecloths and a hostess, having Bloody Marys and a taco salad with a distant cousin whose very existence I'd never even known of a few days earlier. I had only the coincidence of her recent marriage to a close friend of my brother to thank for this—the second marriage for both of them: connections never come easily, it seems, in any part of this family, which seems far more adept at putting an end to things than pulling them together. Like the way my father simply slammed the door on my mother's family at the instant of her death. Pulled the shutters. Cut the phone lines. Stopped the mail.

"I'm sure it wasn't 'simply,'" I said to Debbe, backing off a little from the anger I still feel when I talk about this. I was an infant when it happened, and it was almost twenty years— and then by accident—before I found out about any of it. Of them. That's how good we are at cutting things off. But sometimes the connections come in spite of ourselves. In the midst of this conversation, I had a sudden memory of another meal, in Florida this time, maybe ten years before, with my father, not many years before his death, and his fourth wife. Somehow the story of my mother came up during dessert, and he was explaining to his wife what happened: the caesarian, the septicemia, the demands of her family, the ugliness, the anger, the absolute breaking off, the total silence, and then the complete secrecy, the paternally directed conspiracy of an entire community to bury her name, her memory, as deep as her remains. In amazement, wife number four was holding her fork with the same piece of key lime pie on it in front of her mouth for a good ten minutes.

"I can't believe you did this," she finally said.

I was only listening, like some innocent bystander who had entered the conversation too late to understand what it was about.

"It was probably the wrong thing to do," my father admitted, and for a moment I was about to cry, I think, from hearing this confession, when he added, "But if I had it to do all over again, I'd do exactly the same thing."

Now I was the one who couldn't get my piece of key lime pie to bridge the gap between my fork and my mouth.

"I just can't believe this whole thing," said his fourth wife, who had spent her entire life till then, every day of it until this move to Florida, in Dayton, Ohio, not fifty miles from Cincinnati, from my father's world, from my birthplace and my mother's death place, from this whole debacle.

"I can't believe you didn't know about it," said my father, finishing off his pecan pie à la mode. "Everybody knew."

"Not everybody," I reminded him.

Now my newfound cousin-or-something, Debbe, was expressing her own amazement: "So you never knew anything?"

And, good person that she is, she asked, "What do you want to know?"

REMEMBER THE ALAMO

I wanted to know everything, of course.

So she spent the rest of our lunch together telling me stories. But she is younger than me, the next generation down, in fact. Her mother would have been my mother's niece, her grandmother my mother's sister. While I listened to her, I was trying to figure out the exact name for how Debbe is related to me. I have trouble making these connections, of course; I have always had trouble, ever since childhood, figuring out just how everyone was related to everyone else, once you got beyond first cousins, even in my paternal family, which was the only one I knew I really had. The connections always seemed so fluid that I settled for bits and pieces, for names and faces. But Debbe didn't even have all of those. She tried to enumerate on her fingers the names of the six daughters—my mother, Bess, and her five sisters—but after her own grandmother she couldn't remember. There was the one they supposedly wanted my father to marry after my mother's death—that old Orthodox custom that my father claimed was the source of the bitter falling-out—but she had no idea who this might have been. She charmed me instead by telling me how they all helped their father run the movie theater he owned, where they showed silent films, this sister selling tickets, that one ushering, another one playing the piano, and so on, but she had no idea where the theater was located, where they lived, what became of them all.

Eventually she mentioned that there was someone way back there, a wild one they called him, who had decided he wanted to be in on the settling of the West, who had packed up his wife and belongings and headed for the frontier, who was said to have been at the Alamo. Yes, a wife, too. I forgot to mention the wife. How could I have forgotten the wife? Because they have a tradition of forgetting the wives, in this family, that's how.

Just to your right as you enter the mission complex there is a small room, no more than thirty feet square, where the women and children took refuge during the siege. Is it possible to imagine, even for a moment, that Travis and his men consulted *them* in the process of making the decision to stand fast against the Mexican troops? "Victory," says Travis's final sentence (underlined three times), "or Death." I get the feeling that Travis was addressing that letter via first-class mail—personal courier, certainly—to History. "Fellow citizens & compatriots," its salutation reads. The whole thing has the false ring of pompous rhetoric to it (I know it well; just listen to me, too, trying to deal with history: "the false ring of pompous rhetoric"). I hear the tone of the self-made hero in the process of making himself into a heroic figure: *"Victory or Death."* Was he speaking for the women and children when he wrote that?

Well, he got what *he* wanted, though fortunately, when the Alamo fell, Santa Anna spared the women and children. He even provided them with horses for their exodus. Nothing is said of where they went or who took them in.

Like my mother, they were not part of the story we grew up with, my brother and I. There is a bad contemporary painting that hangs on a back wall inside the Alamo, depicting one of these women riding out through the gates of the compound, on horseback, her baby in her arms and her long auburn hair flowing behind her. It reminds me, as I sit here in the mission garden as the afternoon wanes, feeling the passage from sunlight to shadow, the stone bench cooling, that, thanks to my paternal grandmother's love and perseverance, I have the only two remaining photographs of my mother; I recently had both framed, one to hang on my own living room wall, the other to give to my daughter, who, they say—now that we can talk about these things—looks just like her. I can see that.

The family photo album, on the other hand, the one we had

when I was a kid, was full of blank slots. I used to poke
through it regularly, admiring those willowy, handsome
adults in their twenties bathing suits, their flapper outfits,
their wonderful automobiles, wanting to know everything
about them.

"Who's this? Who's that?"

Uncle This, Aunt That.

And the blank slots: "Where's this picture? Where's that
one?"

It fell out.

So many pictures fell out. How could so many pictures fall
out? All the little black corners were still sticking to the black
pages, but the pictures they had once held had fallen out? I
have a whole huge box full of pictures myself, and none of
them ever falls out, though I once had something of a falling-
out over them. With the woman who was the center of my life
at that time, who came into my study one afternoon and found
that I had been rummaging through that box of photos, that I
had dug out photographs of the two women who had previously been so important to me, both the one I'm divorced
from and the one who died, and propped them up on the
little table next to my desk. She was disturbed. She wanted
to be the only woman in my life.

I assured her that she *was* the only woman in my life.

She was. But I refused to carry on the family tradition and
perform my father's magic act: *The miraculous disappearing
woman! Now you see her, now you don't!* I tried to explain this
(once again), but she was well into her rant-and-rave routine
by then, and there was no stopping her. She paced the study,
swinging her briefcase back and forth. I sat at my desk,
swiveling in my chair. Her voice rose. My explanations fell—
on deaf ears, mostly. She left the room, shouting. I stayed,
brooding. We'd done it again. Eventually, of course, I'd put
the pictures away again. For a while. And then this scene

would recur. It was one of many scenes—by no means our favorite—that we played out over and over again. We were very
good at it; we knew all the lines by heart.

But I was not trying to win any battles there. Only the per-
petual war against loss. Against disappearance. Against the
sad forgetfulness we've always proved ourselves so good at. I
have—we have all, I think—been besieged by a far more powerful force than Travis and his comrades were ever challenged
to stand up against: by nothing less than the most battle-
hardened troops of time, the armed and mounted divisions of
the family itself, the gathering battalions of the past, and all
the massed armies of forgetfulness. We must never surrender
or retreat.

That is what I think, sitting here in the garden behind the
Alamo in the late-afternoon chill. It is midwinter, and the sun
is sinking rapidly now, no longer casting any direct light, any
warmth, upon the garden. The time goes by so fast. You
hardly have time to get anything thoroughly, to get it right.
It's gone before you know it. Earlier, there were children wandering through here with their parents, pointing up at the tall
palms, and blue-uniformed young men and women, admiring
the many varieties of cactus. Now I sit here alone, thinking of
that distant relative, on a side of the family no one ever talked
to me about until just these past two months, who perhaps
wandered through this same compound himself on a winter
day many, many years ago, his wife at his side, knowing that
Santa Anna's army was closing in, wondering what to do. Dis-
cussing it with her, I would like to think. Surely we have been
better, at times, than I have known. Surely we will be better,
at times, than we have been.

So I sit here, still, looking off into the distance toward that
long-veiled side of the family, trying to conjure them again, if

only in the imagination, if only for myself, like a photograph to hang on the wall, if only for my daughter, who so resembles them. Here is Robert Fishbaugh, I think, looking into the shadows across the empty garden. But is it really? "Robert Fishbaugh"? Yes, the names changed, the spellings changed, but does that one ring true? Maybe it wasn't him at all, this Robert Fishbaugh from Ohio-Texas. Maybe he stayed (or became, like so many, as he entered the country) Fishman, just plain old Fishman. It would, I think, have been just like him. And as he and his wife stroll this darkening, chilly courtyard—and is there, also, a child or two, whom they hold by the hand as they walk?—together they decide that it is no longer wise to remain here, with a great, vengeful army descending upon them and an angry, incompetent, self-centered leader in their midst. A Jewish peddlar knows no boundaries. Just as well sell buttons and shoelaces to Santa Anna's soldiers, if it comes to that. For an old-time salesman like Jake Fishman, his territory is . . . the territory. Time to move on. With his wife. With the whole family.

Time, then, to say good-bye to this garden. But also to remember that a farewell is not a forgetting. That there are some times of which we can say, with some accuracy—even if only to ourselves—that we know what we are doing here.

□

## KILLER

Have you ever thought what it would be like to kill someone? I would like to be able to say that although—like the majority of us, I suspect—I may have let the thought surface briefly in a moment of great anger, I've never actually done anything of the kind. On the whole, I'm a peaceful fellow, and though I may merely be deluded by my persistent hopefulness about human nature, I prefer to think the same of you. If like most householders I own a number of objects capable of bringing lives to an abrupt and painful end—kitchen knives, a chain saw, a car, a box of matches and a can of charcoal lighter fluid—I keep no guns or garrotes, no bowie knives, crossbows, bottles of poison. I'd like to say I have no skills in that direction, either, but my brief stint in the United States Army, where much to my commanding officer's chagrin (since I was about to be discharged for poor eyesight) I won a sharp-shooter's medal during basic training, taught me otherwise. Much to my own dismay, it also introduced me to that latent streak of violence that resides in all of us, that potential for, one is tempted to say, anything.

The lesson was simple, unexpected, clean, and over with before anyone, including myself, really understood what had happened. It was a typical spring morning at Fort Knox, about midway through basic training for a group of seriously intimidated draftees in the late stages of the Korean War, young soldiers who had already learned the hard way that pleasing their sergeant had better be the uppermost thing on their minds. They were out of their bunks with their bare feet on the cold wood floor of the barracks before the first note of the recorded bugle call had finished. They'd pissed, washed, dressed, grabbed their (unloaded) rifles out of the rack, and were on their way out the front door for morning lineup while reveille was still echoing around the parade grounds. In a mere six weeks the army had already shaped them into a disciplined group, clearly capable of meeting its standard of instant action without the hesitation of thought.

There was only one problem here: a single narrow doorway for forty troops all wanting to be the first in line in order not to attract the regal wrath of the sergeant. On this particular morning I was in the middle of that crush. I had just made it through the doorway and stepped out onto the little wooden landing where I was forced to hold up for a moment, waiting for others to clear off in front of me, when someone behind me jabbed me in the small of my back, hard, with the muzzle of his rifle. I didn't know who it was, didn't, for even a moment—oh, I was in the process of becoming a good soldier, all right—think, just turned and in one swift motion swung my rifle butt around and knocked the guy behind me into the air, off that little wooden platform and down into the dirt beside the barracks.

You don't know you're capable of something like that until you do it. When you go through life at five foot eight, 135 pounds, you don't go looking for physical confrontations, which you're pretty well assured of coming out on the wrong end of. You keep it cool. Language is your weapon. You learn to defuse, not conflagrate. You never think of yourself as a violent person. You are every bit as shocked at what happened as the guy lying down there in the dirt below you, looking up wide eyed and speechless. The guy you will later overhear saying to some of the most fearsome trainees, tall, muscular guys right out of the Appalachian coalfields, "Don't mess with that

Greenberg; he's a killer." You, the one who can hardly keep a straight face during bayonet practice when you're ordered to scream, "Kill! Kill! Kill!" as you charge the straw-stuffed dummy, won't know whether to be flattered or appalled by your new reputation.

But I never killed anyone. Or expected to. Or realized that perhaps I already had.

The army, in its inimitable and understanding way—based on the it-takes-two-to-tango principle—punished both of us equally. We spent the rest of the long, breakfastless morning shouldering arms and marching around the perimeter of the parade grounds under full packs while the Kentucky heat swarmed up thickly around us and the wind whipped the red-clay dust into our eyes. I considered this entirely just; in fact, I felt I'd gotten off easy for what I'd done. Until that moment, I'd lived under the impression that I was not a violent person.

■

But who, after all, hasn't laid violent hands on the world—or at least felt, at times, the urge to do so? It's not so much the reports of rage on the highways I think about in this context as the rest of us out there in the midst of it with a death grip on our steering wheel as if it were the vehicle's emotions we were choking back. I would like to think that somewhere out there on that choked and choking highway of life there are a few individuals without a drop of aggression in their blood— the Jains of India come to mind, who carefully dust off the seats of chairs before sitting down lest they crush an insect— but I suspect that they're very few indeed, maybe simply better than the rest of us, examples of what we ideally could be, or perhaps just victims of a faulty gene. Our primate genetic disposition argues not only in favor of aggression but also against the survival of those who lack the aggressiveness that was certainly once required simply to stay alive. However well or poorly we manage to handle it, whatever precarious balance we manage to maintain between it and the qualities we're likely to think higher of—altruism, love, generosity, restraint—aggression is surely as innate as anything else that drives us.

So think about it. What would it take, after all, for you to kill someone? Not much, I'll bet. Maybe you already have. Violence is not only our history but also clearly the currency of our age, and the motto on all the coins reads, "Spend, Baby, Spend!" And as you know—if you read the papers, watch television, live in a city, drive a car—we have spent in the proverbial fashion: as if money were going out of style. You may—if you don't drive a car, if you've avoided the military, if you aren't trapped in the inner city—still be hoarding your own untouched lode of violence, but who's to say how long it would take you, when the right moment came, to mine it, mint it, and cash it in? The only question is: what's the right moment? An anarchist mob at your door? The Klan at your neighbor's? A quarrel with your spouse? An attack on one of your kids? A driver who doesn't respect your rights on the highway? A neighbor's pet fouling your garden? The fool who turns the other cheek? What would it take? Passion? Honor? Duty? Money? Or simple necessity? What would it take?

But you don't have to be violent to be lethal. Neglect will do it (forgot to get the kids to buckle up?). Inattention (didn't see that stop sign?). Carelessness (left that campfire burning while you went for a little hike?). Stupidity (kept the gun where the kids could get their little hands on it?). Even good intentions (of course, you meant to get those brakes replaced). And my stepmother—as I did soon after—had the best of intentions when she spoke to me in the privacy of the kitchen one evening while we were washing dishes together (private because it was a place where my father and brother hovered with only hummingbird brevity, for the length of a meal, while she and I lingered to clean up afterward, one of the rare times of usually wordless togetherness I recall from our life together).

Morris Fishman, she told me quietly that evening, almost in a whisper, surely not wanting to chance my father overhearing even from the distance of the paneled den to which he usually retreated after dinner, Morris Fishman, my maternal grandfather, was in the Jewish Hospital nursing home, old and seriously ill.

Morris Fishman: that almost mythical creature from an almost mythical family whose very existence had been raised only once and briefly into the midst of this very material family, like one of those Grimm and horrifying fairy tales from the distant past that had to be told once, informative and cautionary, and then thrust back into the dark forest of disremembrance forever after. Morris Fishman: that despot who like an evil fairy-tale king had so raged at my father's refusal to obey Orthodox Jewish custom after my mother's death by marrying her next available sister (a scurrilous slut, according to my father) that my father (again, according to him) had no choice but to break off all relations with the Fishman family forever after, thus isolating both himself and, not inadvertently, me from the Fishman kingdom. Morris Fishman: not only my progenitor but also, so the tale was told to me, the sole demonic cause of my banishment from the kingdom of my mother's family forever and ever.

But now the implication was clear: with one king in a weakened state and the other no doubt by now snoozing undisturbed in his den with the newspaper over his face, the drawbridge was momentarily down. It was, at last, my opportunity—perhaps my last—to cross back into that forbidden kingdom, if not to reclaim my lost princely status (my ambitions being far too modest for that), then at least to get a glimpse of how life had been lived there all the years of my absence.

Her intentions, my stepmother's, were the best: to give me the opportunity to visit, however briefly, that long-lost realm, to set foot, for the first time, on a small patch of my native soil. And so, I presume, were mine a few days later when I borrowed her car and set off for the nursing home, though whether it was my state of mind that slowed me as I drove across town or the density of Cincinnati's summer sludge of heat and humidity I couldn't say. Nor could I have easily said what, exactly, was on that mind of mine that muggy afternoon as I wallowed, windows down, un-air-conditioned, toward what felt, in some odd way, like destiny: Curiosity? Expectation? A simple desire to say, "Here am I"? The hope for iden-tification and acknowledgment? Fear? The guilty sense that this was an act of disloyalty to the family I'd grown up in? Some of all of that? Or was I just being a good boy and, as usual, doing what my stepmother had suggested?

Killing anyone never crossed my mind; by the time I got to the hospital, it felt like I was the one who was under a death sentence, just waiting for a nod of the king's head to bring the executioner's ax down in its swift descent. I'd already felt par-tially severed from the family I was brought up in by the all too recent news that, in a strange way, it wasn't altogether my family after all. (Well, yes, that news was already a couple of years old and, in the family tradition, successfully reburied by then, but my stepmother's remark over the all too symboli-cally dirty dishes we were washing had brought it up raw and dripping from the grave again.) Now, about to cross this shaky drawbridge—actually just the passageway from the hospital to the attached nursing home—I had no idea what I might be cutting myself off from, what I might be linking myself up to.

It was no throne room I was directed to, though it seemed large enough for a court assembly: a long, wide, white-walled third-floor ward, white curtains drifting as if half asleep in the overheated breeze that shuffled in through the windows and the wide French doors at one end, opposite where I stood, that opened onto a square, low-railed balcony the size of a small room. There must have been twenty beds in the ward, all white sheeted in my memory, lined up in two rows down the long sides of the ward, and in each bed a pallid, old man. Having only recently reread Conrad's *Heart of Darkness,* I felt I had wandered into the white, sepulchral city Marlowe visits at the end of his narration, and instead of the middle-aged nurse descending upon me down the wide aisle between the rows of beds, all in white from her cap to her shoes, might well have expected to encounter those three old women who saw Marlowe off on his journey into the interior seated there staring at me, solemnly spinning, measuring, snipping.

And wasn't it Marlowe, too, whose glimpse into that dark interior let him see what we are all capable of—intentions be damned?

If I wasn't sure what I wanted from Morris Fishman, it was clear from the moment I arrived a few feet from the foot of the bed the nurse had directed me to, with my skinny arms dangling from my short-sleeve cotton shirt, and introduced myself that Morris Fishman wanted no part of me. I'd have gotten more of a reaction by telling him I'd come to change his bedpan than I did by presenting myself as his long-lost grandson. His hospital bed had been cranked up to a half-sitting position—perhaps I'd arrived not long after or just before lunchtime—and he raised his head, white and skeletal, just slightly to stare at (or was it through?) me. But whatever he did or didn't see there, whatever he couldn't bear to see there or preferred not to see there, I was never to know. Without a word, he let his head drop limply back onto his pillow.

Then, as if to make his point, whatever it was—I'll never know—clearer, he turned his head to the side and would not look my way again.

I don't suppose I stood there long. Nothing was happening, nothing to stay for, and I could hardly have marched up to his bedside and grabbed him by his pajama top, demanding that he look at me. We'd both have fallen apart, one physically and at least one emotionally. I turned and left—baffled, relieved, disappointed, all of the above, as before. As ignorant as before of my own feelings, of what was going on here, what this was all about. Nothing much, it seemed. Like a messenger who doesn't grasp the nature of the mission he's been sent on, I must have brought back some sort of vague report to my stepmother, some acknowledgment of what had—or, rather, hadn't—taken place. Not a word to my father, of course. Whatever it was, I knew it was over. I knew I'd never see Morris Fishman again.

But I did hear about him again, and this is both where it ends and where it gets hard—though of course, as we all know, endings are always hard, especially endings that grab you by the collar, as I couldn't have done right in the middle of things with that old man, and pull you up face-to-face with what you've done. Even with the best of intentions.

Within days of my visit, Morris Fishman was dead.

I don't know how I know this. Or, worse yet, how I know the details of his death almost as vividly as if I'd been there—which, in a sense, I had. Granted, almost fifty years have passed since our encounter, but as I've already shown, there are other details of it that I recall with absolute clarity (although, yes, I recognize the possibility of a divergence between my clarity of recollection and historical accuracy). Perhaps it was my stepmother, Zelda, who, at yet another evening dishwashing session—I remember the soft summer light coming through the window over the kitchen sink, but was it that evening or another?—once again brought up the subject of my maternal grandfather. Perhaps there was an obituary in the *American Israelite,* the local paper of record for the Jewish community. Maybe even something in the *Cincinnati Enquirer.* One way or another, the source of my information about the nature of Morris Fishman's demise is no longer available to me, nor has it been, I suspect, since the moment I learned it—and then found it instantly obliterated by the sheer impact of what I'd learned.

What I understood was this: as surely as if I'd been there myself to drag his frail body out of his hospital bed, haul him out through that pair of wide French doors onto the little balcony that opened off the ward, lift him up over the railing at its edge, and drop him onto the pavement three floors below, I'd killed Morris Fishman. That he'd managed it all by himself, that so far as I know my own name never came up in reference to his death, didn't for a moment exculpate me from what happened as an immediate result of my visit.

This isn't just *post hoc ergo propter hoc* thinking.

Sometimes you don't even have to be there to do what you do.

It hadn't been more than a few days since I'd appeared at the foot of Morris Fishman's bed like some unwelcome ghost from the painful past only to see him turn away from me as if I'd slapped him in the face. The next step for him was no doubt seeing that his real answer to my—yes, it had to seem like that—attack on him, my surprise foray across the moat that had safely separated our worlds for two decades, lay in the final turning away. As I reconstruct it, he must have wrangled one of the nurses into helping him into a wheelchair and then pushing him out onto the balcony for a bit of sun. Perhaps he even wheeled himself out there. However he managed it, once

there, alone in the brutal late-afternoon sunlight of recognition, he scooted his chair up to the edge and then, somehow
. . . no, he couldn't possibly have had the strength to do it
himself. As surely as that nameless young draftee those many
years ago must have felt some sudden, mindless force lifting
him off his feet and flinging him into the air, Morris Fishman
must have felt my own hand reaching under the chair from the
back to give him the necessary boost, tipping him over the
railing and, withered leaf that he was, sending him fluttering
down onto the sidewalk three floors below.

☐

# THE EVER-PRESENT

The world is nothing you can get away from. The Segovia concert, the one thing I've found to look forward to here, is a disaster. Probably I shouldn't have come. I am staying with my father and his most recent wife in Fort Lauderdale in January 1978, and I should have known better than to trust them for directions. They haven't ventured more than half a mile from their retirement condo since they moved here and as far as I can tell don't intend to; Miami itself is still a foreign land to them, and not just because of their fear of Hispanics. They barely know where it is. The directions I get to this concert hall to which I shouldn't have come are like those you'd give a kid to tell him where to look for the Big Dipper: up. In this case: over there.

But that's not all. Three days here and I can already see that my father's not his old self. He stays away from joining the regular gin rummy in the downstairs card room with the other old guys who live in their building, although ever since I've known him, which is to say all my life, he's played twice a week and won a few bucks far more often than not. His explanations to both them and me are vague. And we have to be in the condo at certain times of day so he can see his programs, this man who all his life could no more sit through a TV program than an opera. His programs are all soaps. We rush back from an early lunch to *All My Children,* and he's too absorbed in it to even explain to me what's going on. (I can't help it,

I'm still like this: if the TV's on, if it's going to thrust its follies into my life, I've got to know what's going on; otherwise it's like trying to watch a ball game without knowing the score, the inning, how many on, and how many outs.) And lunch, speaking of follies. I thought we were looking for a restaurant, but it turns out he's looking to see where his wife went and with whom, so every day we're in and out of three or four restaurants till we "accidentally" run into her and some of her women friends. But no one will give me any credence when I point out these strange behaviors, which are tearing at my already shredded heart and which, it eventually turns out, are the first signs of his deterioration, the results of some small, unnoticeable strokes.

Meanwhile, when I decide to get away from daytime TV by going down to the pool to sit and read in the chilly midwinter sun by myself, I suddenly find I have company. My father and his wife have these neighbors, a couple they go to their terrible early-bird dinners with every evening—every afternoon, actually—where they eat the kind of gummy food you can otherwise get only in TV dinners (and that I eat with them, of course, cleaning my plate like the good boy I've always been, which isn't all that difficult because in spite of the texture of things long dead, it doesn't taste bad, in fact has no taste at all). And these neighbors have sent their also visiting son, who's a famous diet doctor, down to keep me company by the pool. It's like there's some kind of agreement to send the kids—some kids!—outside to play together. And this chubby boy-man, his pale belly bulging over the top of his bathing suit, is squatting beside me so that I have to move out of his shade to retrieve my bit of sun, and he's rattling along with this theory of his, which is about as credible as I'm already suspecting his diet program is, about how the dead are hovering around us all the time. This I do not need to hear. I am here only in the hope that the world will leave me alone for a little while with my own grief.

So when I see in this morning's *Herald* that the famous Andrés Segovia, the man himself, is giving a concert tonight in Miami, I think, This is exactly what I need. I will sit in a darkened concert hall and listen to the delicate hands of this amazing musician, whom I have only ever heard on recordings, picking out Bach preludes and partitas. I will let myself sink into the quietude of that precise and beautiful music, and, for a little while at least, the rest of the world, including what is grinding away inside my own sad self, will go away.

This is, of course, a delusion.

My getting there we won't even talk about. It's winter dark already by the time I set out in the Cadillac that's rusting away from salt air in the condo garage because my father, the lifelong traveling man, suddenly doesn't like to drive anymore either (he has me drive us on our lunchtime expeditions; their friends drive us all to dinner). I don't know my way around Miami at all, having been here only twice before in my life and never having left the oceanfront either time. Help is not exactly forthcoming. I hesitate to ask the friends because pretty soon we'll have everyone in the high rise debating how to get to this place where none of them has ever been.

But I get there all the same. Sanity and the rational life may have deserted me these days, but my sense of direction, for some reason, is still hanging around. I am like a wounded bird whose navigational system is still sufficiently intact that he can handle migration; my bad wing is constantly dragging me off course, but gyroscopic mechanics keep compensating for my drift. I get there, even though I don't know where I am, couldn't point out the spot on a map of Miami though I am a devotee of maps. I even find easy parking on the street. I've never had a problem showing up at the last minute and

getting a single ticket for anything, and this time is no exception: I get a good seat toward the front of the balcony and am
nicely settled in there as the hall lights begin to go down.

It is a magical moment. In the darkened concert hall where
eyes haven't yet had a chance to adjust, suddenly a single spot-
light, like a window blind snapped up in a shut-in's room to
show what a glorious day it is out there, picks out an empty
chair in the center of the stage, an ordinary, nondescript
wooden chair against which a guitar leans upright. Hardly a
heartbeat later, Segovia steps into this brilliant splash of
white—a small man, I think, though I can't be sure, given my
distance from the stage, the angle of view, and the lack of figures of comparison—dressed in a white suit himself. He picks
up the guitar and takes his seat and . . . and three people are
pushing their way through the darkness into my row, so that I
have to stand up to let them pass, and by the time we're settled again, the music is already under way.

I'd like to tell you what the master is playing, but I'm too
distracted by the people talking a couple of rows behind me to
give it my full attention, and, of course, turning around to
glare in a totally darkened hall accomplishes nothing, though
that doesn't keep me from trying. I'm lecturing myself, instead, about patience, never much of a virtue of mine, but by
the second number people are still arriving, stumbling down
the steps to the first section of the balcony, causing a great
shuffling of skirts and jackets and feet and programs. People
are popping up and down all around me, as if the seats have
been fitted with randomly activated springs. Off to my right I
can detect at least two separate conversations, and to my left a
watch alarm dings—once, twice, three times. A couple of
minutes later, like a delayed echo, another responds from just
behind me. We have our own chorus up here in the balcony,
voice and percussion, while down on the stage this tiny man,
without the aid of a microphone, alone in a circle of white

light and concentrating his entire immaculate being on the instrument he holds across his lap, is delicately picking out the notes of something it's become totally impossible to pay attention to.

I'm too polite. I wait till intermission to leave my seat, though by then, of course, I'm ready to barricade the doors against latecomers, gag everyone within twenty rows of me, and rip watches off wrists. Still, they've kept coming in; they ignore both their musical time pieces and the music I presume they've come for, but not each other. I try to convince myself that it's the insult to this great musician, an old man now whom none of us is going to get to hear perform much longer, that's got me so pissed off, but I know deep down that what I'm even more angry about is not how they're obliterating Segovia but how they're intruding on me.

Down in the lobby I push through the crowd to the ticket window and demand my money back. I paid to hear Segovia, I say firmly, and this is what I have to listen to, explaining. Much to my surprise, the ticket agent slides a twenty across the counter, beneath the bars. He shrugs, tells me it's like this all the time, what can you do? I'm standing there thinking of a few things I could suggest, but he's already turned back to his bookkeeping.

And so I'm standing in the street outside the concert hall just like that, even more frustrated. I was at least expecting to vent my anger with a good argument at the ticket window. But now I'm stuck with this young evening that's already ruined, sunk many fathoms deep by the noisy storm that's behind me now, and I have no idea how to go about salvaging it—or me. Back already to my father's condo, where they have the famous, fat diet doctor's book prominently displayed on the coffee table, seems like a depressing idea. But disoriented and not wanting to get seriously lost, I get in the car and allow my unconscious but vaguely reliable sense of direction to guide me meanderingly toward the Miami Beach area, till eventually I end up pulling into the parking lot of a bar that looks like a pirate ship that's been driven ashore here by the last hurricane. It appears tipped to one side, and I haven't even had anything to drink yet. I hate to think of what it must be called. I go in and sit under drooping fishnets at the long bar, which is totally deserted. I order a bourbon on the rocks from a bartender wearing what's supposed to be a pirate's puffy-sleeve white shirt and a black bandanna tied around his head, and look around me. There doesn't seem to be another customer in the place. And now the bartender is nowhere to be seen. It's so quiet you can hear water dripping off the glasses drying in their rack down at the far end of the bar.

Distract me, I'm perversely thinking now. Someone, please, come and distract me. At the moment I'd settle for some sloppy drunk in a stained linen jacket, his wide floral tie pulled open at the neck of his unbuttoned shirt, sliding onto the next bar stool and offering me lukewarm portions of the mushy TV dinner of his life story. You know who I mean, the heavyset guy with the long ash at the end of the cigarette dangling from his wet mouth who's always pushing in at the crowded bar between you and the person you're there to enjoy the evening with. Where are they when you need them? Okay, he's a stereotype, but I'm no longer looking for art this evening; my fellow concertgoers have already torpedoed that ship—I'm just looking for entertainment. And it doesn't even have to be all that entertaining—just distracting. The cliché that dynamites a work of art just greases your way down the mindless slide of entertainment.

"How's the weather down there?" my friends in Minnesota ask when I call to check in.

Not what you think, I want to tell them.

I tell this old story (which still feels tongue-burningly hot off the grill in spite of the lukewarm taste most of that week served up to me) in the present tense, as if it's happening in our now instead of its two-decades-ago reality, because the world's intrusions are, in fact, ever-present. That's an amazing term, isn't it: *ever-present?* *Ever-present* is not memory, which is a catalog of the past you can call up as cheaply and easily as an 800 number where the clerks are on duty twenty-four hours a day to take your order, where sometimes you get a busy signal, of course, sometimes the lines are down, sometimes, as the recording says, "We're sorry, but that number is no longer in service," and frequently the UPS man will arrive several days later with the wrong product, but you get my point: it's out there, back there. The ever-present, on the other hand, is not out there; it's right here. It's . . . ever-present.

There's considerable disgust on the literary front these days with the use of the present tense. Some consider it a sleazy and already-tired trick, an aging magician's attempt to hype up the action when he knows the audience has already fallen asleep on him and won't even notice that what he's pulled from the hat is a dead rabbit. William Gass is especially severe: "The present tense is a parched and barren country," he writes in *Finding a Form,* a place doomed by "its limited scope and its absence of mind." Worse yet, he tells us, it's a kind of literary sickness: "There is a lot of it going around," he worries, and "what was once a rare disease has become an epidemic." On the other hand, even he admits that it "is the condition of a verb," and therefore what we say in the present tense "will remain in the present tense through all eternity"— which is exactly my point here, in this here, where its ever-present intrusiveness gives us not only what intruded in that long ago past but also the power that intrusions have to stay with us, if not "through all eternity," then at least through that minimalist version of eternity we call our life.

The beauty of the present tense is that through its verbal sleight of hand (which, like most skills, is undoubtedly capable of abuse: the electrician who can wire his way around the burglar alarm, the high-wire artist turned second-story man, the novelist turned political speechwriter), the past, which is always with us in deed, because who can unhappen it, is also always with us in word. "Once a thing is known," Anita Brookner sadly refrains in *Look at Me,* "it can never be unknown. It can only be forgotten." True enough, but if I'm not mistaken, not forgetting's exactly what a lot of this thing we call writing is all about: keeping *it,* as best we can, the *it* that was and always will be, present. Plain talk tries for it, too. The linguists even have a term for it: *historical present.* You've done it or heard it yourself. In the midst of relating what happened earlier in the day, you find yourself saying, "So I'm in my car cruising down Main and I see Tommy on the other side of the street, so I pull over and yell at him. 'Hey, Tommy,' I say,"—and you see how it goes, presently.

For some, though, this is an intrusion: a latecomer stepping on their toes as it squeezes by to its seat for a show it hasn't got the smarts to understand, music for its tin ear. They're offended: is this really necessary? It's spoiling the performance for them. They want their money back, and who can blame them? They came here to get away from idiot intrusions like that, and look what happens! Haven't we all known for a long time now that "the world is too much with us; late and soon, / getting and spending . . . "?

Well, I don't know about that "too much" part: when does quantity spill over into unbearable quality? But yes, the world most certainly *is* with us (and give special note to the present tense here, how it seems perfectly okay for the poet—no fair!): the world like an out-of-control, run-on sentence full of party crashers with their big feet and self-absorbed conversation and noisy paraphernalia—watches like crickets, pagers like front-door buzzers, beepers beeping and cell phones like a whole rhythm section of bell ringers—but also the drunk whose obnoxious breath you were hoping to find in your face when you needed him, but who's instead fallen asleep in his Buick with its wheels over the concrete stop block in the parking lot, which is too bad for you but lucky for someone whose windshield he won't be intruding on when he wakes up at first light sober and too hungover to do anything but drive straight home.

It's the arbitrariness that does you in. Why can't these people just mind their manners (literary manners, too: the past tense was good enough for Dickens, good enough for Dostoyevsky)? I'd like to know too. I want my money back! Not just the twenty I already got (that was almost too easy, almost like being ignored), but also the plane ticket (not cheap, either; it's high season) that got me into this, and compensation for the early-bird mush someone else has paid for and *All Someone Else's Children* and the lunk getting between me and my sun at poolside, and these are nothing, really, they're just . . . pimples, they're not even boils, but they're here—then, now, always, what's the term again? *ever-present*—and the variation on Robert Graves that Stanley Elkin reiterates throughout *Pieces of Soap* is right: "the *Book of Job* is the only book."

There are no bombs falling here, no minefields to walk through on the way to work, no toxic wastelands where the children play. There are no soldiers armed with automatic weapons stationed on the street corners. In my neighborhood, at least, we do not hear the sound of gunfire in the night (though, according to a police department mapping of gunshot incidents that I recently saw in the newspaper, the major concentration of such events in my city is no more than half a mile away). The sirens that scream with some frequency through the busy intersection nearby are on their way to the usual urban crises: car crashes, kitchen fires, heart attacks. They are reminders, of course, of what can happen anywhere, anytime, to anyone, but so far, I'm happy to say, they are not pulling up in front of my house. Day or night, we walk the streets without fear. Though perhaps I risk the wrong people learning about this, I am known to go off leaving the doors unlocked. The sky is not falling in.

So what difference, really, do the world's daily intrusions make? Twenty years after that abortive trip to Miami and this evening of my life is a lovely concert I've had to make a long and difficult drive to get to. Okay, I was slow arriving, but I'm here now and enjoying it. So what if the other latecomers are beeping and buzzing, if some jerk cuts too close in front of me on the interstate, his right signal light blinking not my annoyance but his, if yet another telemarketer who can't answer a simple question about his own product calls just as I'm sitting down to dinner, if the chain saw, like some balky child on the first day of school, won't start on the one day I've set aside to clear deadfalls, if colleagues oblivious to their own deep-seated personal problems choose me as the canvas to splash their ugly abstract expressions on, and the one I love no matter what leaves her muddy socks to dry on the dinner table . . . oh, I could go on and on, and so, I'm sure, could you. But what's the point? We're all like Beckett's man dying of cancer who's obliged to consult the dentist for a toothache. These things happen, but they're not our life—or, as the case may be, our death. In what we might half-jokingly and altogether solipsistically call the great scheme of things, they don't really matter, do they?

Well, no, but also yes. If a life like a book has a theme, they're certainly not it. If the issue is one of character, these things are outside the self, not inside; they touch but don't enter. On the other hand, theme is a kind of summing up, a sort of life after death—what comes to mind after you close the covers on the book for the last time—while these intrusions are the altogether too lively and relentless stuff of the day-to-day; there is no summing them up except to say they keep on coming. And character may in part be defined by how we react to them. Intrusions, one might argue, are where the action is; they are (not only but also sometimes overwhelmingly) what's happening. In their ever-presence is where we find the stories of our lives. Not the generalizing "I'm a traveling salesman" (who isn't?), but specifically, as a friend reports, "Almost as soon as we were off the ground, this perfectly ordinary-looking woman, in her forties maybe, dressed in a nice gray suit, started in on me with personal questions: Was I happy in my life? Was I satisfied with my income? How was my health? Before I knew it she was pushing these incredible brochures on me. . . ."

Me, I'm flying the no-small-talk flag from the moment I find my seat: a book, a newspaper, open in my face as soon as I've buckled my seat belt, a notepad on which I will in all likelihood note nothing lying on my lap. We do what we can to ward off unwelcome intrusions, pulling whatever accoutrements we can cushion ourselves with down around us like mosquito netting. And still we're aware of the angry buzz of the world going on all around us: the little kid just behind me kicking rhythmically at my seat back, the hulk in the aisle elbowing me in the head as he tries to cram his steamer trunk into the already packed overhead bin above me, the late-boarding passenger shrilling at the flight attendant about her God-given right to a window seat, inhuman voices quacking over the intercom—are our seat backs upright? are we sure we're on the right flight? has anyone brought a bomb aboard? Did someone say *bomb*? The world *is* too much with us.

Unlike Job, however, it's not our faith that's being tested in, say, a darkened concert hall, where we're attempting to pluck out a delicacy of guitar strings from among the jingling of electronics and the jangling of bracelets, vocal vibratos, and the swish of silks, but our endurance. Stanley Elkin's fixation on the Job story is certainly understandable; for someone in the late stages of MS it must indeed seem that everything intrudes upon the ability to do anything. But for any of us, the question some days—and perhaps it's largely a matter of our sensitivities at those particular times—is: How much can you take? How many hang-up calls, "Fatal Error" messages, unexpected bills in the mail, embittered coworkers, broken fingernails, sick dogs, "Road Closed" signs, unanswered messages, hairs in your coffee, lost car keys, and Jehovah's Witnesses ringing your doorbell can you handle before it seems as if it's not just the day but your life that's being over-whelmed?

Some days even start off like that. Witness Nathanael West's Miss Lonelyhearts:

> For a little while he seemed to hold his own but one day he found himself with his back to the wall. On that day all the inanimate things over which he had tried to obtain control took the field against him. When he touched something, it spilled or rolled to the floor. The collar buttons disappeared under the bed, the point of his pencil broke, the handle of his razor fell off, the window shade refused to stay down. He fought back, but with too much violence, and was decisively defeated by the spring of the alarm clock.
>
> He fled to the street but there chaos was multiple. Broken groups of people hurried past, forming nei-ther stars nor squares. The lamp-posts were badly spaced and the flagging was of different sizes. Nor could he do anything with the harsh clanging sound of street cars and the raw shouts of hucksters.

What a mess. Perhaps it's only the bad dream of the privileged, of those who aren't preoccupied with where their next meal is coming from, where they'll sleep tonight, what will become of their children, when the assassins will break down the door, when the next bomb will fall; but still, if it's what's happening, it's what's happening. One way or another, the world, which there's no getting away from, has the capacity to break your heart, sometimes shatteringly, sometimes just by grinding you down. The thing about the world is, it just keeps happening. There is no bomb after all (not here, at least), but nonetheless small, sharp-edged, armor-piercing fragments of the world are flying all about us, and the only defense against them that I know—though a sense of humor surely helps—is equanimity, a word not much in vogue these days and a quality not readily come by. I think I could maybe name one or two friends who have managed to set up housekeeping under the shelter of equanimity, but I have seen the holes in their roofs, too, and I have seen them shiver in the cold rain that comes leaking in.

But maybe that's what equanimity is: not seeking shelter from the world, but achieving the ability to go on living in the downpour without drowning in it. Acknowledging its ever presence—and your own. It may be what's happening, says the equanimitist, but so am I. And so, then, is a lot more. Because if you can do that, there is no limit to what you can do. In which case the only question is: how do you get to the point where you can do that? Where you can look at the boils on your arms and the crops rotting in your field and the broken timing chain and the faddish oaf trying to lecture you on the spirit world and—without whining "Why me?" or joining the conspiracy-theory club or plastering a cynical "Shit Happens" bumper sticker onto your forehead—slather on the cortisone cream instead, curse the weather, stick out your thumb, keep your nose in your book, get on with your life?

Equanimity knows that it's not over till it's over and that between now and then, no matter what's always happening, anything can. And only by understanding that it can is there a chance that it will. And only by understanding all that can equanimity be achieved. Circular logic, but given the alternatives, given what's happened and keeps on happening, it's not a bad circle to be caught in. There is presence here; here it is always the present. It is where, in spite of everything, you can hear the music playing.

□

# HERE AND THERE

Pilgrimages seem to be almost instinctive, or at least derived from behaviors now so ingrained in our species that it's difficult to distinguish between genetic and social origins. Of all the animals that migrate, we are surely among the most restless. But humans retain the influence of the geophysical habitat in which they pass their formative years. And often, it seems, we are drawn back to our childhood homes—if not physically, then mentally; if not out of love, then out of curiosity; if not by necessity, then by desire. Through such returning we find out who we are.

—John Janovy Jr., *Vermilion Sea: A Naturalist's Journey in Baja California*

The myth of the boy running away to sea is famous among us. Melville's Ishmael, its prime avatar, demands to know, "Why is almost every robust healthy boy with a robust healthy soul in him, at some time or other crazy to go to sea?" Richard Henry Dana, who dropped out of Harvard to ship out on the appropriately named brig *Pilgrim* as an ordinary seaman, serves as its foremost literary purveyor in *Two Years before the Mast*. And nineteenth-century tales of boys who ran away to sea are legion. But in fact I know two twentieth-century men, "inlanders all" as Ishmael would have it, who did exactly that. Make that three, if I'm to believe my father's self-mythologizing. And all three of them, not surprisingly—perhaps implicitly acknowledging Ishmael's recognition that "If they but knew it, almost all men in their degree, some time or other, cherish very nearly the same feelings towards the ocean with me"— fled the landlocked Midwest.

One, the younger of those first two—I'll call him Skipper for the fact that he goes by a nickname and because the sea became, finally, his vocation—came from a little town in central Wisconsin, a land of small lakes where he grew up watching and dreaming of the grace of sailboats. The other, now aging—let's call him Frank for the bluntness of both his name and his character—was a Minnesotan who grew up along the north shore of Lake Superior, which provided him with at least a vision of the sea (albeit an inland one) before he dropped out of school at sixteen, during World War II, and ran off to Seattle to join the merchant marine. But he came back after the war, hard of hearing as the result of a bomb explosion aboard his ship, to cling as grimly as lichen to the same rocky shore he'd left behind. As did Skipper, to build a home with a crow's nest view on a high basalt dome overlooking that same inland sea.

And then there was my father, three times a runaway, to hear him tell it, on each occasion to water, twice to sea. And always, after, back to his childhood—and adult—home, back to Cincinnati.

What is one to make of all these men in flight? But maybe Ishmael has already answered that at least as well as any of the sociologists and psychologists who've set sail on the murky seas of that same male journey in our own time: "It is a way I have of driving off the spleen, and regulating the circulation. Whenever I find myself growing grim about the mouth; whenever it is a damp, drizzly November in my soul; . . . then, I account it high time to get to sea as soon as I can."

Perhaps the more intriguing question is: what is one to make of their—our, my—returns?

■

Unlike those men in flight, those sailors and slip-aways, I have always wanted to be—and to know—where I am. I've flown, but I've never been in flight. I won't deny that my move to graduate school in Seattle was motivated in part by the desire to get as far away from Cincinnati as possible while still remaining in the continental United States, but it was more complicated than that: with two young children and another on the way, Skipper's kind of flight, or Frank's, was neither desirable nor possible. I took my little world with me wherever I went. I have circumnavigated the globe, in the process of spending a Fulbright year in India, but I was always aware that the end point of that was to get back to where I'd started. And the people I met in India were even more intense and specific about that sort of sense of place: they didn't want to know where I had come from (the United States, Minnesota, St. Paul: merely obvious data); they wanted me to name for them my "native place" (Cincinnati—and this wasn't data but bedrock reality, however slow I was in coming to understand their sense of belonging, of identification with place, and maybe also the fact that, in the process of India's becoming a more mobile society following independence, the sense of place, of where one truly belonged, where one was originally *from*, was becoming ever more fragile and important). They would define me, and have me define myself, as they defined themselves, in terms of some deeper sense of where—and therefore who—I truly was.

My very own relentless concern, the one that thumps along with me like my heartbeat wherever I am. Location, location, location: my own slogan long before real estate agents began to harp on it.

I always keep a U.S. atlas in the trunk of my car, maps of various states in the pockets behind the front seats. I open airline magazines to study the route maps in the back, even the diagrams of airports. Call me obsessive, but I can't pass a map without stopping to examine it. In London many years ago, as I entered Hyde Park Zoo, the diagram displaying the layout of the grounds brought me to an immediate halt.

"I thought we were here to look at the animals," said my snide and sometime girlfriend.

"The animals are where they are," I told her. "I want to know where *I* am."

In fact—and perhaps in contrast to the runaways (although even they probably do know, to their dismay, exactly where they are even while they're searching for the quickest route out of town)—I suspect that's what most of us want to know, and I often find myself acting on that suspicion. I love it when people stop me to ask for directions, even in the midst of one of my long, sweaty runs, where they're costing me precious time; even in strange cities, as happened to me recently in New York, where I'm as ignorant of the terrain as they but flattered, nonetheless, to be mistaken for someone who *looks* like he knows where he is.

For many years I have been something called a section leader, a volunteer position, for some six miles of the Superior Hiking Trail (SHT), a gorgeous ridgeline forest trail that parallels the north shore of Lake Superior. If you're ever in northern Minnesota and in a mood for a hike (and why else would you be visiting here?), this is the place for you, these hundred miles and more of sometimes rugged and often panoramic trails between Duluth and the Canadian border. And surely one of the things you will want to know, aside from identifying the local flora and fauna, is where you are. This, of course, is where I come in. All along my section of trail I nail what we call assurance markers at eye level into the sturdy trunks of maple and birch and balsam: little three-inch-by-five-inch plastic rectangles bearing the SHT's blue, green, and white logo. You can't miss them. I tack them up everywhere, with far greater frequency than my job description calls for. I may not be able to provide you with latitude and longitude (though I see more hikers out there every year who share my concerns, toting global-positioning satellite devices), but I can still make sure that you know you're on the SHT. I can assure you that you are not lost.

And we have those larger signs out there in the woods, too, especially on the cross-country ski trails, the ones with my all-time favorite phrase on them: YOU ARE HERE. Accompanied, of course, by a red dot or a small, swooping arrow.

And this, I think, Keats aside, is all you know and all you need to know.

This is not a metaphor.

On the other hand, I don't have anything in particular against being lost. I have been seriously lost (in a very real, physical sense—don't talk to me of metaphysical mazes, of misdirections of the mind and the strange labyrinths of the heart) three times that I can recall, once in the north woods, twice in urban wildernesses. But it was a lovely, mild autumn afternoon in the woods, and though there was no trail to follow and no assurance markers held my hand from tree to tree, I had water and snacks (a candy bar for me, a biscuit for the dog), the birches and maples were just beginning to turn, there was nowhere else I needed to be (nor anyone who knew where I was), and I was depressed, so being lost didn't seem like such a bad thing after all. Also, though I was in a wild, rugged area of some tens of square miles, it was, I knew, enclosed within an equilateral triangle of three roads, nicely distributed: one county, one state, and one federal highway. Since no one was likely to be looking for me, I wasn't at all sure that was going to do me any good, but it had a nicely symmetrical feel to it all the same. Obviously if I could keep going in a reasonably straight line, I'd eventually find myself standing in an overgrown roadside ditch somewhere, among cattails and faded fireweed, but equally obviously, given the terrain—steep hills and broad swamps—there was no chance of my going in much of a straight line. Need I mention that I didn't have a compass? I did have the dog, though, my overweight yellow-lab mix, Sonny, who finally, as if in disgust with my ignorance or impatient with my maundering style, put his nose to the ground and led us out over what even I, after a mile or so, began to recognize as the same route we'd taken in.

I don't much get off the trails anymore, and certainly wouldn't do so again without a compass (and a dog), but that hasn't stopped me from cutting loose in the city, where the roads are everywhere and clearly marked, and getting equally lost. The homunculus of an adventurer in me seems to insist on turning my long runs into this sort of thing from time to time, though unlike those legendary men who would rather spend their lives as automotive Flying Dutchmen than pull into a gas station to ask for directions, I'm never adverse to seeking a bit of help. The goal, after all, is to end up right where I started.

When my father was a young man, or so he once told me when I was even younger, he left home for San Francisco, where he signed on or was, as the expression went, shanghaied onto a tramp steamer for a voyage to Hong Kong. He was not one for the rich details of storytelling, however (a trait he shared with the rest of the family, perhaps under the assumption that if everyone just stays home, as this family has mostly done, then everyone knows the same stories already and there's nothing that needs to be retold), and the contextual evidence fails to support his story. He has also explained how he dropped out of school at sixteen to go to work, became a salesman first, then a dealer in real estate, was socially active in Cincinnati—a swinger, I think a later era might have called him—and by his mid-twenties was married and ready to settle into family life.

But suppose this story of his adventure at sea were true. Did he run away without so much as a scribbled note left on the kitchen table, or did he depart on his youthful travels with his family's blessings and a reminder to call home collect? (Not for a moment can I believe that my grandmother would have approved of this, who never quite forgave her younger son for moving fifty miles away to Dayton, Ohio). What was it like, that Pacific crossing, that strange new world of ship and sea and the distant Orient? Did he return out of a sense of familial obligation, with the satisfaction of mission accomplished, with the relief of having escaped a maritime kidnaping, or feeling somehow defeated, disappointed, with the proverbial tail between his legs? None of this was ever forthcoming. Perhaps it was only a story he made up to amuse a child, not unlike the bedtime tall tales about strange creatures and their midnight adventures that I used to tell my own small children; or to bolster his own image, to replace, in his child's eyes—or his own—the staid and settled businessman with an image of exciting masculinity. My brother recalls having heard this same story, but is that evidence of its veracity or only of the fact that our father had few stories to tell and a love of consistency?

The second time he took off was true blind flight, motivated by grief and despair following his wife's—my mother's—slow and painful death in 1932 from a childbirth infection, an agony that wound this inexpressive man tortuously tight and then sent him spinning away on a two-week binge not to sea but to one of America's great water spots, Niagara Falls, where one can only speculate that he'd honeymooned with her. This time it was his sister's husband who eventually tracked him down, bailed him out, and brought him back, hungover and disheveled and disoriented, the details of his flight lost in his brief, alcoholic erasure of memory.

It was his second wife's death, three decades later, that sent him back to sea again. But he was nearly sixty then, long settled, retired in fact, still in his native place, of course, no longer the impetuous young man who might or might not have wrangled his way onto a rusty old freighter without a passport or an able-bodied seaman's papers. And maybe there was a tinge of guilt or obligation here, too, not just the "need to get away" he mumbled about to me some weeks later, but a need to honor his second wife as he'd done his first, though without the drinking—he'd hardly had a sip in all that time since. He called his travel agent and booked a Caribbean cruise—round-trip airline ticket to the port of departure, needless to say—and who could blame him?

Following my own loss (Wendy Parrish's tragically young death from Hodgkin's disease), though not, I think, following in his footsteps—I didn't so much want to go away as to be somewhere where I might briefly feel I belonged—I went to spend a week with my father where he was then living at another of America's famous watering spots: Fort Lauderdale. But I couldn't stand it, couldn't stand the feeling that I didn't belong there either (in what seemed like a transplanted Midwest, among all those retirees clinging to each other in their displacement from their northern homes), couldn't take any pleasure from their wintry sun and sea, their all-day gin rummy games and early-bird dinner specials, couldn't wait for the week to be up so my flight could take me back to what still was, however empty, home.

It's not that I'm afraid of water or uncomfortable on boats. I was a freestyler on my high school's championship swim-

ming team. I'm at ease boating on the Ohio River with my
brother, though it's also worth noting that in spite of its sleek
lines and twin 240hp Chrysler engines, the boat is called
*Going Nowhere* (and is named after my 1971 novel of that title,
lest I give the impression that I'm a latecomer to this concept
of staying in one place—the here rather than the there). And
that going nowhere—that is, sitting tied up at the dock, serving as a floating living room, sun deck, and wet bar—is
mostly what that boat does. And that it does that—where else
but?—in my native place, that complex and conflicted, ever-
so-difficult-to-negotiate, little metropolis on the banks of the
Ohio.

Because of all the hills around which any journey has to be
negotiated, there are usually three or more ways to get from
anywhere to anywhere else in Cincinnati, not counting up and
over. This is a city of villages connected over time in all the
odd and angled ways villages connect, not unlike, say, London,
in its conglomerate structure. No urban plan was ever laid
over it because there never was, until much too late, any "it"
to subject to the grid of a Chicago or Manhattan. Its multitude of parts just grew together as they grew individually over
the decades, the centuries. Some of them never did get incor-
porated into the city proper that now surrounds them, leaving
them islanded, a Norwood or St. Bernard, inside its municipal
boundaries. And others that did join the city still retain their
own clear identities, of which they have become increasingly
proud of late, posting decorative signs along their thorough-
fares announcing their names and in some cases the dates of
their original founding: Columbia-Tusculum, 1788. They are
what they are, and, for the most part, proud of it. No one, not
even a stranger, would ever mistake Mt. Adams for Mt.
Auburn, Price Hill for Bond Hill, Paddock Hills for Walnut
Hills, though there is no more a walnut to be found in the one
than a paddock in the other. Nor would even a visitor from

another country, or another world for that matter, mistake old Porkopolis, the once-upon-a-time Queen City of the West, for either of her shabby Kentucky handmaidens across the river, Covington and Newport.

The roads, anyway, follow the hills—or the limits the hills impose upon them—and more: they follow the banks of streams that have long since gone into hiding in underground conduits; they follow old wagon roads that once wandered from one village to the next; they follow trails the Miamis laid down centuries ago and long-abandoned deer runs and, who knows, maybe even the paths the mastodons trampled through these once-forested hills on their way down to the big river. Today the roads scurry between the hills, wrap themselves around the hillsides, leap across the little valleys on slender bridges, or plunge right down into them. They end abruptly at heavily wooded ravines, suddenly change direction and sometimes even names as the topography dictates, and in a few cases meander up the valleys and around the hills and through the former villages until at last they find their way out of the city. But the one thing no Cincinnati street ever does for long is run straight and true, and that might even be taken for a significant indigenous trait, not to be separated from the complexities of the city's service as a way station on the underground railway; its German, Jewish, black, and Appalachian ethnicity; its conservative-leaning-toward-right-wing political mentality; the northern consciousness that informs its southern exposure as it looks across the river to the Kentucky bluffs on the other side; the fact that people in the East think of it as a midwestern city while those in the West consider it eastern; and maybe, too, the great meandering Ohio itself as it snakes its wide way under the shadow of the city's hills along the course of an itinerary that carries its waters all the way from the Allegheny Mountains to the Gulf of Mexico, a lengthy, muddy, and indirect journey by any measure.

I wrote that description of Cincinnati in a "story" once, a work of fiction; in fact, those are the story's first paragraphs, and the story itself, which is about nothing if not the uncovering of one's sense of place, is premised, as I discover in rereading it, on a series of mercifully unstated clichés: No matter how far you travel, there's no place like home. "Home is the place where when you go there . . . " "Where the heart is . . . " And so on. How tedious. How true. Yes, travel is broadening—as we know, there's a trite saying for everything —but only when you settle down do you get a deepening.

"Why am I here rather than there?" is my version of Wittgenstein's famous "Why is there something rather than nothing?" My own "heres" may be multiple—I have had homes both in St. Paul and on the north shore of Lake Superior—but the evidence of my attachment to both of them comes when I approach either after a time away. Coming up over the rise on U.S. Highway 61, just a quarter mile from that northern home, I experience a sudden rush of mixed feelings as I lift my foot from the accelerator for the downhill glide toward the gravel driveway: the elation of arriving again at a place I know and love, but, at the same moment, a fear for it: What if something's happened—if it's been burned to the ground, blasted open by a tornado, vandalized? What if it's not there?!

And the same thing happens each time I return to St. Paul, the moment I slide down the Victoria Street exit off I-35 and swing around and up the curving city street that will take me home. I won't exactly say I hold my breath—too clichéd, too impossible for that many blocks—but . . . I hold my breath. I need that quick peek down Lincoln Avenue to the third house on the right, the bright flicker of its pink porch door an antidote to my vision of its charred remains, before I can ease the car a half block farther to make the turn into the alley and reach up to click the garage door opener clipped to the sun visor.

With what relief am I, finally, there. I mean here.

■

In spite of my own landlocked, stay-at-home proclivities, I have nothing against those who choose the life Conradian or bicoastally Kerouacan, or who, like Bruce Chatwin, define their lives as an *Anatomy of Restlessness*. I've been on the move enough myself as the twentieth century's version of the itinerant scholar took me from Cincinnati to Seattle to Mexico to Lexington, Kentucky, to India and St. Paul and Boise, plus the usual travels that go with the territory: for conferences, research, lectures, artists' retreats. And yet I would say I've never been restless—except when I've been away from home and restless to return: anxious, once again, to confirm with my own eyes that the home place is still standing. Nonetheless, I have the greatest admiration for Skipper's captaincy of oil tankers and Frank's merchant-marine service. And my own father: how can you not admire the adventurous spirit that took him across the wide Pacific—or if not that, then the dream of it that rejuvenated him decades later? And my grandfather. And my great-grandfather. Ah, the family travel stories.

My father's father, born (in Ukraine) and bred (at the Cincinnati Art Institute) an artist, abandoned his life as a painter to hit the economic glory trail of the roaring twenties, heading, of course—how they all do it!—for water. He opened a resort hotel in Miami Beach, just then in the process of blossoming into America's vacationland, though the killer frost of November 1929 soon wilted that bloom—and his hopes— and sent him scurrying back to Cincinnati. In spite of the drastic financial setback, however, this was not an altogether unfortuitous return. My grandmother, delighted to be back from a "there" she only ever after mentioned with sneering disdain to a "here" where she felt she and her family truly belonged, was perhaps the only person in the nation to take solace from the stock market crash. (And in semi-ironic moments during which I envision another such crash as the only event ever likely to reassemble my own grown and scattered children in my household, I acknowledge my heritage.)

Still further back down that same generational line my great-grandfather was in flight as well: from persecution in nineteenth-century Ukraine and probably in fear for his life, and in his case not so much to the sea as across it; not from the Midwest, obviously, but to settle in the Midwest: that place, the very city, which not only somehow called to him but seems, since, to call us all back. And then there was that story of someone even further back, on my mother's side this time —that Robert Fishman-Fishbaugh—abandoning his home to fight at the Alamo: not gone to water, this fellow, but gone once again from the Midwest. Evidence is lacking here, and the timing renders it unlikely, but I've recently found it recorded that someone from his neighborhood and his ethnic group did (a sizable neighborhood, however, that southern corner where Ohio and Indiana meet along the river, although a tiny ethnic group at the time, those Jewish settlers). One way or another, it's an interesting if apocryphal tale, in some ways not unlike my father's. Did he really go? If so, what motivated him? And what happened there? But, more to the point here, did he ever return? Not many did from that particular debacle. And if he were there, and if he survived, would he have returned, or would he have gone on, instead, to California, say, if not to meet the Pacific, then perhaps because his adventurer's ears were panning the first trickle of news about the impending gold rush?

No one, after all, thinks of Cincinnati as the center of the universe, at least not beyond those early childhood years in which one thinks—with considerable insight and accuracy for that particular period of one's life—that wherever one is is the center of the universe. And yet I too am subject to whatever gravitational pull drew my great-grandfather to it, my grandmother and my father back to it, has held my brother captive to its magnetic force all his life. I can think of less than a handful of years in the four decades since I moved away from there in which I haven't made a pilgrimage . . . home, I'm tempted to say, long as it's been since I've actually had a home there. But if *home* isn't quite the right word, *pilgrimage* does seem appropriate. And though no one, I think, would categorize Cincinnati with such holy places as Jerusalem, Mecca, or Benares, still, the places that draw us so regularly back to them, as this one has done to me and mine (both my sons live there now, back in the city where they were in fact born, their native place), partake somehow—the rationalist in me resists the word *mysteriously*—of that power.

But it's a mixed blessing. Unlike the other homes I travel to, I never wonder, as I roll down the winding hills off I-74 into the Mill Creek Valley or watch the descent across the wide bend of the Ohio River into the Greater Cincinnati Airport (which, somewhat disquietingly, isn't even located in Ohio), whether it's still going to be there. I know the pleasures of those arrivals. I know the genuine warmth of the welcomes I'll receive from my family there, and from their old friends and mine. I know the comforts of familiarity: old neighborhoods, specific places, certain foods (need I pen a sacred hymn to the butterfat content of Graeter's ice cream, to the idiosyncrasy of Cincinnati chili?). One doesn't even always need to taste such exotic manna; one feels blessed simply to know it's there.

And yet. John Fowles has put it best for me in his "Notes toward an Unfinished Novel" when he speaks of entering upon certain scenes, certain places, certain people, where he must "become mixed in their lives and social routines," where he knows that in a sense he belongs and yet cannot help feeling like a visitor from another planet. "I like earthmen," he admits, "but I'm not quite sure what they're at." He is engaged, amiable, understanding, and yet, he concludes, "we regulate things better at home." And so for me there is a certain excess of materialism, of acquisitiveness; there are extremes of racism, sexism, and homophobia that I am unaccustomed to— restaurants that one does not go to because of their sizable black clientele or their gay cooks (AIDS from pasta?)—though I also know how much more extreme that was when I lived there; there are ethnic assumptions (of superiority, mostly, and of the role of women) that it seems to me no rational person could subscribe to; there is a chillingly reactionary political climate that gives me the shivers even during the hot and humid summers of my visits. Even the city water is unpalatable. And yet I drink it. I drink it all in, though it always leaves a slightly bitter aftertaste in my mouth. Perhaps it's the sense that overall, in spite of a slight easing of racial barriers here, a new riverfront development there, an updating of the water treatment facility, nothing really changes.

And perhaps that's the way it's supposed to be in whatever passes for our sacred places. If they changed, after all, would they be, any longer, the places they were, the places that sucked us back to the sweet-and-sour nourishment of their breasts? If Jerusalem were Tel Aviv, if Mecca were Beirut, if Benares were Bombay and Cincinnati were New York, they wouldn't be Jerusalem and Mecca and Benares and Cincinnati any longer. They wouldn't possess what they'd always possessed to draw us back, to welcome our return, to leave us feeling as if we both belonged . . . and yet no longer belonged, as if we were both native and alien at the same time. As if this were not the very state of our lives wherever we find our place in them.

□

# SILENCINGS

My cousins, it turned out, didn't even know there'd been a poet in the family. It was only one of my father's terse, acidic slogans, "No good"—a label he applied to many a man and woman who passed through his field of vision but never, of course, explained (what more was there to say? if someone was "no good," then that someone was no good, the label was the life, and that's all there was to say about it)—that had ever given me, decades ago, a clue about the existence of this literary ancestor. And I was never sure even then whether this comment on my great-grandfather was intended as a judgment or a warning. It was, perhaps, only information, offered as an expression of my father's awareness at the time that I myself was showing some suspect interest in such literary arcana as poetry. But what information! Another poet in the family! Where? When? What? Who was he? I needed to know.

Imagine: almost to the age of independence in that environment, and I still hadn't caught on about silences.

There are silences, I have since learned, and then there are silences. At the far left end of this spectrum lie, sometimes not so quietly, the silences willed or chosen: the monastic's attuned only to the voice of god, the criminal's or spy's ("I'll never squeal"), the lover's cold shoulder or deaf ear from which no entreaty can summon forth a sound, or those practiced and calculated silences of the men of my father's generation, modeled, perhaps, on the terseness of the legendary westerner who had more important things to do than talk, for whom talk was a wasteful, trivial, womanish sort of thing. My first wife's father may well have had good reasons for choosing his particular silences. As the white pharmacist who owned a drugstore that very likely dispensed more than just prescriptions (medications without prescriptions? numbers? secrets? it was all a secret) in the all-black, residential Sterling Hotel in Cincinnati's no-longer-extant West End ghetto, it might not have been a healthy thing for him to have talked too much about what went on down there.

For my own father it *was* just a matter of prescription, and his simple prescription was, "I don't bring the office home with me." And he didn't. He flew his own flag—his personal equivalent of "Don't Tread on Me"—and he lived under it. All our pleas to know what he did all day long at the Monte Casino Wine Company fell on deaf ears—or, rather, a zippered mouth. Those were the years of World War II, and you might have thought he was living by one of that era's famous mottos: Loose Lips Sink Ships. The federal government, as I later learned when I went to work for him, did in fact try to silence him once, attempting to strip him of the very name of his company following the bitter, costly battle at Monte Cassino during the Italian campaign. But when action was called for, he was able to speak up loudly and clearly on behalf of his business, and so managed to retain his rights because of the difference in spelling and the fact that his bottling plant was actually located on the site of a former monastery of that name.

Among the family, however, silence reigned, nor was it possible to know why he really chose it. Did he think that what he did all day long was too trivial to be worth talking about? Or was it too important? Or did he think that we, his wife and two sons, were incapable of understanding it? Surely he didn't think we were likely to betray his business secrets, assuming there were any, to his arch rival across town, the Gibson Wine Company. Maybe it was just, in his mind, "man stuff," the serious business of the world and therefore a separate category from the world of home and family, from any world outside the world of work itself. Anyway, it was a willed silence, it was a silence he willed, and he was a willful man.

He had, in fact, a number of such flags he flew in lieu of conversation, not unlike a ship running the black-and-yellow quarantine flag up its mast, a bright, lucid burst of communication saying, with as much force and conciseness as possible, Stay Away. When he announced every four years that "what this country needs is a businessman for president," he wasn't opening up a discussion of the current political milieu. He was quite simply stating all there was to say about it. He had nothing more to add to that, and if you thought you did, well, silly you. You weren't about to get another response out of him. And when he announced, as he frequently did, in both the best and the worst of circumstances, that "everything works out for the best," you were only wasting your breath if you wanted to know, "What everything? What best?" He'd already said everything there was to say on the subject. He had spoken, true, but his words were like scissors that had snipped a huge hole out of the very center of the delicate fabric of communication that stretched between us, and left, hanging there by the thin thread of a trite slogan, nothing. A silence. Chosen. Willed. His.

I am not, I'm happy to say, my father's psychoanalyst—or anyone else's—so I can slip rather quietly myself away from any analysis of his silences simply by saying that I'm sure there must have been reasons for them: societal reasons (but he was *Jewish*, denizen of, as Stanley Elkin has put it, a culture of "Criers and Kibitzers"), professional reasons (but he was, in good part, a *salesman*, that is, a talker by definition), personal reasons (but he was pleasant, reasonably gregarious, even charming—people *liked* him), who knows, maybe even genetic reasons.

And I am, as that last category denotes, my father's son. I know silence. Silence is a part of me. I have been born and bred to silence. I may not have any flags I can wrap myself in, slogans to enforce or account for my own silences, but they're there. They have, I often feel, been enforced upon me, and it takes an act of will to disentangle myself from them, to speak through them. They are the silences I would unwill.

At the far right end of the spectrum of silences are those that are not willed or chosen but inflicted: the traumatic forces or physiological factors that strike some people dumb, the to-talitarianism that sentences the outspoken to gulags of silence, the censor prowling the stacks and the airwaves with gag in hand, bonfires and fatwas and Indexes, family secrets. It's one thing to hush a child interrupting adult conversation, to whisper, "Quiet, please," to the person behind you at the concert, to ask a whole audience to hold its peace while the speaker has her say or to hold your own until your friend's had hers—these are silences that probably fall somewhere in the middle of that spectrum, negotiated silences—but it's quite another to slap a strip of duct tape over your victim's mouth, to verbally slash and burn your way through the garden of someone else's speaking, to vacuum the very words, like breath, out of a poet's mouth.

There were, in fact, a few fragments of information, or what passed for it, about my father's father's father, the poet, that I did, in time, manage to chip off that wall of silence, not all at once by any means. Where did he come from? Russia. Where in Russia? Russia. When? Back then—what difference does it make? And? A peddlar; he was a peddlar. I mean his poetry. Hebrew; he wrote in Hebrew. What was it like? Pastoral; he was a pastoral poet.

Well, that was something, at least in the way of evidence

not only that I had a vaguely remembered great-grandfather, but also that he had actually been a poet. "Hebrew" and "pastoral," language and genre, nothing my father was likely to have invented even if he had been the sort of person to fabricate stories, were sufficiently specific to add up to some degree of probability. I chose not to pursue the question of pastoral, my father not being a literary man and my own image of a Jewish pastoral poet being somewhere in the realm of the fantastic. But Hebrew, that sounded (though it later proved false) reasonable. And I had a name, too, by then, even a pen name, Dovid ben Yishai, to go with his actual (that is, Americanized) name, David Greenberg.

What I didn't have were the poems.

"Where," I wanted to know, "are his poems?"

No poems. Lost. Gone. Forgotten.

"He published them?"

Nod: yes.

"Then someone must have them."

No. No one.

We were sitting in my cousin Mary Lou's house, in Dayton, many years later, long after my father's death, having Sunday brunch, my wife and I and my two cousins and their husbands, all of us except my wife rather getting along in years ourselves by then, when it first came out that neither Mary Lou nor her sister, Carol, knew that they'd had an ancestor who was a poet. Not until I had returned to the area in that January of record-breaking cold and snow to try, finally, after all those years (going on half a century of them) to find those poems that I'd been told no one had, had they ever heard—not from their mother, my father's sister, not from our shared grandparents—that another poet had preceded me in the family.

Talk about silences.

We were sitting around the coffee table, enjoying mimosas

and each other's presence, looking through the family photo album that the two of them had assembled from every old nook and cranny of the past they'd been able to mine, when we came across a sepia-toned photograph simply labeled "Grandpa Ben Greenberg's father." A very elegant photo it was, too: a mature, bearded, tie-and-jacketed man, with a high forehead and a wide mouth, one closed hand resting against his left cheek, the other holding open a book on what appears to be the edge of a table.

"Those are your eyes," said my wife. (Oh, that Mongolian, oh, that Greenbergian, epicanthic fold.)

"That's him," said I.

Only by picking steadily and frustratingly at the solid brick wall of my father's, and the family's, silence had I ever gotten any opportunity at all to peek through the tiniest of chinks into my great-grandfather's world. And until that moment, there had been . . . no one there.

But there most assuredly was someone there: at his funeral, according to the headline on the obituary I finally found in the Yiddish-language *Jewish World,* "Thousands of Jews" attended, including half a dozen eulogists: a rabbi, a doctor, a lawyer, and an editor among them. Hardly the kind of crowd you'd think would gather to say farewell to a man who was "no good."

And there was also, I found as I continued my research at the American Jewish Archives and the Hebrew Union College Library in Cincinnati, a respectful listing for this heretofore invisible—indeed, practically nonexistent—man in the *Concise Dictionary of American Jewish Biography:*

GREENBERG, DAVID (PSEUD = Ben Yishai)
b. Volhynia, 1852; d. Cincinnati June 22, 1917. To
US 1885. Yiddish poet, composer, Cincinnati. See
AJYB, 20 (1918-19): 218; Eisenstadt, 30.

And in those two references as well: the *American Jewish Year-book* and Eisenstadt's *Hakme Yisroel be-Amerika.* Plus two brief obituaries in the *Cincinnati Enquirer* and two more quite expansive ones in *Die Yiddische Velt.* The data—dates of birth, immigration, and death; last home address—don't always precisely agree (though all accurately indicate a widow and four [adult] children left behind), but his presence, the fact that he truly was someone, registers well up on the decibel level in that vacuum of family silence. Even the cosmopolitan *Enquirer,* Cincinnati's daily paper of record, acknowledges him as a "widely known . . . writer of poetry."

So what happened? Where did he go? Where did his *poems* go? What worse fate can there be for a poet, after all—for isn't poetry itself the art of witnessing, speaking out, honoring, retelling, remembering, memorializing?—than to have a spell of silence laid on his poems? To be deprived of what is finally a poet's most precious quality, his own voice? Who would do such a thing, and why? How did it all get to be lost and forgotten, the "no good" poet himself disparaged, practically obliterated from family memory, to the extent that his children and grandchildren rarely even spoke of him and his great-grandchildren, my cousins, knew nothing of his existence, when poetry itself, as I've written in a poem of my own that tries to pay tribute to him, is "the only antidote we've got against that deep forgetfulness"?

To write is to break a silence; to publish, to cast one's voice out into a still larger silence. Every word that blackens the white page inscribes the writer's voice against the world's blank, surrounding silence—against, sometimes, the static of its white noise. The scratch of a pen, the click of a key, is like a pecking at the shell of the world into which the writer is forever struggling to be born, to take wing, to sing out (for let's not forget that that biographical entry lists him as a composer as well as a poet). What sort of world is it that instead of listening for these possible musics casts its steel net of silence over such a frail thing as poetry?

For starters, I discovered, one that doesn't like the poet. Oh, not the world at large, which is rather too much to either blame or rely on, but the world close at hand, the world that can feel us, touch us, listen to us, the only world that can really take us by the hand and keep us from passing into oblivion—or, conversely, with its own reasons, legitimate or otherwise, let us go, perhaps without even waving good-bye, without, needless to say, a final word of farewell.

And the deeper I dug, the more I began to see that perhaps they did have their reasons, that family, for letting David Greenberg slip from their grip and, along with him, the poet Ben Yishai, easing the one into the grave and condemning the other to silence. Or perhaps it was the other way around, a desire to bury the poet, finally, and let the man slip silently into his eternal rest. It wasn't because he was a bad man—a genuine thug of a "no good," a gambler, a drunk, a wife beater—that they so readily relinquished him, but, in fact, because he was . . . a poet: a poet among people who had no place for poetry's noisy babble in the midst of the concentrated silences they were intent on focusing on the task of making their way in a new world. In such a context, there was no place for poetry's presumed distractions from the serious business of life.

It was the getting on with that serious business of life that weighed against David Greenberg, finally, and I suspect that no matter how many poems he laid in the balance on the other side of the scale, or how much acclaim they brought, no matter how many mourners gathered at his graveside, or how many editors found him worthy of biographical inclusion, he'd still have been found wanting.

*Williams' Cincinnati Directory,* an annual publication that began in the mid-nineteenth century, a kind of local census that lists, by street address, each adult resident, along with occupation and business address, if any, does a fair job of tracking his career, such as it was. He first appears in it in 1883, the year of his emigration (alone; his family, his wife and three young children—the fourth was born soon after—joined him the following year) from the province of Volhynia in the

Ukraine, as a "bunch breaker" (the worker who rolled the first strips of tobacco in the cigar-making process), then for a long time as a peddlar, for a couple of years as a dealer in notions and candies, eventually as an optician, once in his later years, oddly, as a correspondent, and then one final time as a peddlar again.

Peddlar: that classic occupation of the eastern European Jewish immigrant.

You wouldn't find a poet shucking work clothes at the end of the day and announcing, "I never bring the office home with me." You won't find a poet leaving the office behind; wherever the poet is, that's where the office is. So you might have found him laying his peddlar's pack down in the corner of the rented house after a week or two on the road—not sufficiently lightened, perhaps, of its load of homely items: needles and thread and thimbles, eyeglasses, buttons and scissors—and picking up his pen. It's not by walking the lonely roads from one Ohio Valley farmhouse to the next that he's become, as another bibliographical entry puts it, "1 of the best

SILENCINGS

Jargon [Yiddish] poets in Cincinnati." On the other hand, it's
not by writing all those poems, by becoming, as his primary
obituary in the *Jewish World* puts it, "one of the most popular
Yiddish poets in America . . . [whose] songs were printed in
all the major Jewish newspapers in America," that he's been
able to support his family in the manner in which they had
doubtless hoped to become accustomed in the New World.

Because one of the things *Williams' Cincinnati Directory*
makes clear is that he's not done a very good job of that. Not
only does it record his long history as a peddlar (1884-1897),
while others of his ilk were piling up their small profits so
they could trade in their walking shoes for white collars and
open the little dry-goods stores that some eventually turned
into department stores, even great chains of stores, but it even
gives evidence that when he finally did settle down as an "optician," at 1419 Elm Street or 414 Armory or 735 West Seventh or 759 West Court, his home address and place of business were always the same: not exactly a sign of prosperity. In
fact, the directory lists a dozen different addresses for David
Greenberg between his arrival in 1883 and the turn of the
century, twenty-two between his first listing and his last,
thirty-four years later, in 1917, the year of his death, at 242
Fosdick Street in Mt. Auburn: a pretty steady average either
way of a move about every year and a half.

And what is one to make of that, even of the fact that most
of those addresses lie within a radius of half a mile, that some
are even on the same block, except that old dilemma of the
impoverished: eviction. No one moves that often by choice,
nor do those changes of address equate, say, with Cincinnati's
version of a climb from the lower to the upper East Side. It all
speaks to one thing. As does the record that by the beginning
of the new century, his four children, all adults, are still living
at home. Poverty. One can only wonder why, given that
record, the two sons are listed after the turn of the century as

artists, careers that in the end profited them no more than poetry profited their father. (Of the two daughters, one appears briefly as a "tailoress," the other for several years as a "saleslady"—neither of them the occupations of a rising middle class—before both disappear into the name changes of marriage.)

Only in the final year of his life does the poet (no occupation listed) finally rise from the downtown urban ghetto, never more than a mile from the river on the Ohio's broad floodplain, to the heights of Mt. Auburn: to his death from, according to his Certificate of Death, a cerebral hemorrhage, at that Fosdick Street residence where his widow, Minnie, remains for another seven years before departing, very likely with the assistance of her children, for the newly developing suburbs further north.

■

So who was it who decided, finally, to leave my great-grandfather, his life and his work alike, behind, back in the ghetto of forgetfulness, as the family, most of it anyway, climbed up, north in the way we read our maps, out of the valley of poverty, toward success and the suburbs, toward the good life? Maybe time itself is the greatest silencer. But only if we let it be. More often, it takes a little more human intervention than that—understandable intervention, even, in the flight from poverty: the haste to leave all that, and the who and what were responsible for it, as far and as fast and as fully behind as possible. Maybe even to leave some human token behind, a sacrifice to propitiate the jealous gods of success.

Because David Greenberg's oldest child, Abraham, one of those two sons listed as artists, was another who never managed to climb the hills that ring Cincinnati's river-level downtown. Once, on a sweltering summer day in my early teens, accompanying my father on some unmemorable errand, he surprised me by driving well out of his usual way into the midst of what was by then a ghetto of Appalachian immigrants clustered at the foot of Mt. Auburn in their flight from rural to urban poverty. The streets were lined with men in stained undershirts, smoking, silent, with women in flowered-print dresses, as gaunt as the men, except, often, for their bellies, and with children everywhere, barefoot, half naked, dirty. Here he finally stopped, engine idling, in the middle of the street, in front of a derelict-looking building squeezed in between a boarded-up hardware store on one side and the filthy, jumbled window of a drugstore on the other. He flipped his cigarette out his open window and then leaned far over to point out the window on my side of the car: "Your grandfather's brother lives there."

My grandfather has a brother?

Talk about silences.

At street level, through a begrimed plate-glass window— did it still read, in peeling gold lettering, "Cincinnati Sign Company," the last address, at 29 East Liberty Street, that *Williams' Cincinnati Directory* includes for him before a final brief move to the Jewish Home for the Aged?—it was just possible to make out a sparse display of artist's materials: a thin pile of sketch pads, a few paint tubes, scattered brushes and pencils. Memory plays tricks on me here; for a moment I imagine myself inside the store, peering through the smeared glass of display cases at fine-tipped brushes and boxes of charcoals and curling sheets of drawing paper that have lain untouched for years, while slowly, from the back, a stooped, old man with hair like a scattering of dust balls picks his way across the warped wood floor toward me. But it never happened. The Oldsmobile's engine idled impatiently, midstreet. We didn't linger long enough for me to measure the layers of dust on that window full of art supplies.

My father, as usual, accelerating smoothly away from all

that with his whole generation's Hydramatic drive toward success, had the final, the silencing, say: "He's a failure."

I was never quite sure, back then, what to make of that little side tour. A warning? An object lesson? My own immature ambitions as a visual artist were soon enough to uncover my inadequacies in that area anyway, just as my solid middle-class upbringing was to guarantee that I'd never let myself deliberately risk sliding back down the hills my father'd so successfully climbed onto that old Ohio River floodplain of poverty, particularly the artsy sort.

What does belatedly occur to me, though, is that it was an explanation of sorts: This is why we do not talk about those people. This is why they have been condemned to silence. So that we may speak with confidence in the world we've arrived at, we must let the world we've come from lapse into silence.

Let it, hell. Make it.

Because this is the word from the hills: If the price of poetry was poverty, then the price of poverty is silence.

It wasn't, of course, the poetry in the man that could be silenced—according, again, to that obituary in the *Jewish World,* my great-grandfather was still writing poems even on his deathbed ("one of his last songs that he wrote for this newspaper was a song of joy and consolation, a greeting to a free Russia")—but the poetry he left behind, and ultimately the man himself: sentenced to silence by a society, a family, that judged him wanting, found him a failure, labeled him "no good," wiped the slate of family memory clean of his existence, rendering the man and his work alike invisible to succeeding generations. Except for that one small smudge of a slogan: that no good, that failure.

But sometimes that's all it takes. Perhaps there's always a trace of erasure left behind, a palimpsest, a faint echo in the silence, a finger trailing in the dust, pointing the way. And if we look behind that smudge, that heavy-handed erasure by those who'd wipe away what they don't, in their devotion to the serious business of the world, find worthy; if we listen for the sounds they've tried to silence in their memory and ours, what do we see and hear but a whole world, every bit as real and serious as theirs, trying to speak out to us, to call us back to it, to remind us how much it has to say to and for us, how much a part of us and our world it is: the voice of the dissident, the bleat of some endangered animal, the distant davening of the crypto-Jew in the deserts of New Mexico, and, not least of all, the poems—for I've found them now—of my great-grandfather.

☐

# SHIRTS AND SKINS

As a young man, recently out of college and the army, recently married, I put on a suit and tie and went to work for my father at the Monte Casino Wine Company, the boss's son, serving as liaison between the office and the plant, handling the payroll, the incoming orders from our wholesalers, shipping schedules, and billings, and occasionally even going out to the loading dock to help stack a semi right up to (and sometimes a little over) the legal weight limit, with thirty-two thousand pounds of cases of gallons and half gallons, fifths and quarts and pints and half pints, some of them straight off the bottling line and, as I clutched them to my chest, still warm from the pasteurizer. It was a job, a job I learned quickly and easily, a satisfactory job, and I even came to love the heavy, bittersweet, winey odor that flowed out of the storage room with its rows of five and ten thousand–gallon holding tanks and through the bottling rooms and even seeped into the paneled office I shared with our secretary, a rich, heady smell that I still carry in my sensory memory more than forty years later. But it was not a job I was ever comfortable in.

There were a lot of reasons for that: boredom with the repetitiveness of it, with the rigid hours, the long daily commute, the weekly payroll, the monthly inventory, the quarterly ATF reports, the regular visits from the glass salesman, the label salesman, and the advertising salesman; the lack of intellectual challenge once I'd constructed a more efficient system of processing orders; and probably just my square-peg-in-a-round-hole self. But one of the major discomforts, the one that in the solid family tradition for dealing with difficult issues I kept trying to ignore, deny, suppress, or otherwise evade, never with complete success, was that I knew what that stuff I was ordering the glass and labels for, scheduling the bottling of, sending out on the trucks, and doing the billings for was, and I knew where it was going.

What it was was fortified wine, wine that had been raised from its normal fermentation level of 12 to 13 percent alcohol to 20 percent alcohol by the addition of brandy. It came in all kinds of flavors—muscatel, Tokay, port, sherry—but, though I used to take a bottle of sherry home now and then to use in cooking, it wasn't anything you'd want on your table with dinner. What it was was a cheap drunk: eighty-nine cents a fifth in most stores back in those days. And where it was mostly going, after it had passed through a pair of middlemen, the wholesaler and retailer, was the ghetto: not the suburban Jewish ghetto where I lived, understand, but the downtown black ghetto, the black ghettos of Cincinnati, Columbus, and Cleveland, Indianapolis and Louisville and elsewhere: where the retail buyers weren't the advance guard of America's more recent love affair with the grape, weren't interested in the bouquet, in the hint of pear or cinnamon, but only in how much and how cheap and how reliably the same from one bottle to the next; where our customers were, to be blunt about it—because this was the lingo of the times that we were all fluent in—winos. Mostly black winos.

That was the run-down neighborhood where my discomfort resided, where my conscience wandered lost through dank tenement hallways.

Here we were—here *I* was!—engaged in a business that should have turned my ethical guts inside out, given what I'd long since seen.

In my first job, at age sixteen, I'd worked Saturdays as a

stock boy at Ben's—Ben Schottenstein's schlock house on the edge of Cincinnati's West End ghetto—stocking bins of cheap crap for his always poor and mostly black customers who could afford nothing better than cheap crap and who were sadly happy to be permitted to pay for it on Ben's famous "lay-away" plan, which, though I didn't think much about it at the time, probably allowed them to pay twice as much for the cheap crap it was a crime to be selling them anyway. All of which provided my boss, Ben, a respectable Jewish business-man from my own neighborhood, with the Lincoln Continen-tal he once gave me a lift home in and the other luxuries of his comfortable life.

But we are such slow learners.

After my two years of watching firsthand just this one ex-ample of those millennia-long victims of persecution and racism so readily turning into racist persecutors themselves, preying for profit on the ghettoized blacks of urban America as relentlessly, if not so violently, as they themselves had been preyed upon for all those generations by Poles and Russians and Germans and . . . take your pick, and then seeing the same principle underlying my own daily work life, I should have gagged at the first sniff from that powerful vintage drifting in to me from the bottling floor.

Of course, we were nicely distanced from it all at Monte Casino. At Ben's the customer was always in front of you, se-lecting the flimsy shirt, the poorly stitched pants, hauling the shoddy merchandise off to the layaway counter, getting screwed right before your very eyes. The customers *we* were in immediate contact with, on the other hand, were the nicely suited white gentlemen we mostly dealt with via the telephone who ran the wholesale distributing companies; even they dealt only with the retail store owners, not the ultimate customers, so we were doubly insulated. It was no problem for my father, a man of otherwise unimpeachable ethics, whose easy answer about what I was beginning to consider a very dubious business was that if we didn't do it, someone else would. I had no doubt about that; plenty of others were already doing it.

And I was one of them. One with the Jewish slumlords (but at least I didn't have to penetrate the yellow stench of those decaying, overcrowded buildings to collect the rent); one with the Jewish insurance salesmen trekking through those same miserable hallways to pick up the quarters and dimes that never paid up those meager policies; one with the Jewish housewives bobbing their noses, dyeing their hair blonde, and employing underpaid black "domestics" to labor in their homes. The fact is that if we hadn't been Jewish, the ethical dilemma would still have been there. But the fact also is that we were Jewish; we were, as I kept being reminded, the Chosen People, but I didn't like the fact that what we were choosing to do could shame the *lahmed vov,* those thirty-six unknowingly good men on whose existence the world depends, out of their innocence. (How do I, apostate, know about things such as the *lahmed vov*? From reading, of course. In spite of everything, I love those Jewish writers, their knowledge of kabala, their crying and kibitzing, the way they toss those Yiddish phrases around. But I'm embarrassed by them, too. Grow up, I want to say. You're a third-generation American. Be a . . . *mensch.*)

There's more than enough irony here, I thought, more than I could bear then in the prospect of history's perennial victims turning into present-day victimizers. Some days at work I found myself detecting underneath that rich, winey smell that pervaded my life a rancid hint of hypocrisy.

Slow learner that I was, it took me half a dozen years to decide to opt out. Sort of. Ethical dilemmas seldom succumb to the Gordian knot solution.

At dinner some years back when we were talking about the history of difficult relations between Jews and blacks, a black friend of mine, the poet Michael S. Harper, stunned me by saying, "The problem started when Jews decided they were white people."

I don't remember how the conversation went after that, or what, if anything, I said in response; sometimes recognition does that to you: shuts you right up. There isn't anything to say or do except nod your head and eat your vegetables. Later you can start wondering when and how that strange phenomenon happened. Looking at my bare forearm laid on the dinner table next to my wife's pale one, it's pretty obvious I'm not what anyone with halfway clear vision would call white, no more than Michael is black on any color chart I've ever seen. But that sort of recognition has been around for a long time, and Michael's comment on color certainly dug more than skin deep: because color and the uses to which it is put are wholly matters of who is doing the defining, what today's theorists would call the cultural construction of color.

I've recently heard on the news, for example, about an Egyptian, now a naturalized American citizen, who's gone to court to get himself declared African American, reportedly to be able to take advantage of affirmative-action policies; U.S. law currently defines people of Egyptian ancestry as white, no matter the shade of their skin or the continent they've come from. Color, it would seem, exists not in the eye of the beholder but in the letter of the law, which encodes custom, defines culture.

So it's not hard to imagine that when the diaspora scattered those darker-skinned Jews across northern and eastern Europe as strangers, as outsiders, the natives, who constituted the power structure and were therefore able to set the rules, had no problem defining them, establishing the differences, putting them in their (outside) place: These people are not like us; they are not white people. Therefore they cannot live in these (our) neighborhoods, they cannot own this (our) property, they cannot hold these (our) jobs, they cannot receive citizenship, cannot, cannot, cannot; those things are reserved for white people, like us.

In the New World, however, where sizable numbers of Jews eventually began to come in flight from all that and in search of a new life, they must have sensed that one of the things they could now do was to start anew in more ways than one. Like so many other immigrant groups from the very first—the Irish, the Italians, the Lebanese later, all of them initially labeled "nonwhite" by the British and northern Europeans who had preceded them—now they had the opportunity to remake themselves, to define themselves as they preferred, not as others had defined them: Hey, look at us; we're white people now. The corollary, of course, was that to make that distinction, someone else now had to be the nonwhite people. Native Americans for starters, but they were fast disappearing. Meanwhile, of course, the nation had long been busy importing the people it would force to do the white man's work for the white man's profit and live the way the white man wouldn't.

For the Jews, then, it must have been a little like choosing up sides for a game: No, I'm tired of playing on that team, they're always losers. I'm going to be on this team now. Like "shirts" and "skins" in pickup basketball, and we know who got to put on the shirts and who got defined by their skins. But it was no game. It was terribly desperate if anything, an act of survival that announced, We cannot live, cannot be treated, like that any longer. You have to have a lot of sympathy for those who struggle to redefine their position in the world. It isn't easy. And it's not without consequences for others. Nor is it without consequence for themselves, once a generation or two has passed and they begin to take the shirt for the skin, to believe in the myth of their whiteness, both to take it for granted and to begin to exercise the power it grants them—which, given how color is both determined and determining, is the power of the dominant society. Long before Michael's illuminating comment, I knew I didn't want to be a part of that.

■

On the way out, it felt to me as though it was enough to be able to say, only half jokingly, that some of my best friends were Jews. It was, at least, the truth.

I wasn't much of a young Jew, anyway—though it fell to me as the older son to accompany my mother to temple on selected occasions since my father wouldn't—and I never wanted to be an old one. There are, in fact, only a few things that will drag me into a house of worship of any denomination: a wedding, a funeral, or an aesthetic occasion, which is to say if it's the venue for a special musical performance or an architectural marvel in its own right or home to some noteworthy works of art. I don't celebrate the High Holy Days, I didn't raise my kids as Jews, and I don't have much sympathy for the way the Israelis deal with the Palestinians, to say nothing of that long, dismal history (interrupted in the sixties by the bright flash of support for the civil rights movement) of how Jews have dealt with blacks in this country, more often than not by making money off the very fact of their oppression.

God I'm not acquainted with.

When I'm confronted with the not-infrequent questioner asking me if I'm Jewish, I find myself pausing before answering. Am I? Well, in the eyes of the world, where these decisions seem to be made, I suppose I am. I'm not ignorant of the fact that, instead of the gold stars I was getting on my grade-school work sheets in the late thirties and early forties, had I lived in Europe I would have gotten instead a yellow star, a trip to one of the camps, and no chance to ever utter these protestations of conscience. So, in spite of having long since granted myself a divorce from the faith, I nod. Which seems to be all my interlocutor wants from me but doesn't answer the question to my own satisfaction. Am I really? If I reject so much—so much behavior, in particular? If I see the connection as an affront to not just my atheism—who cares about that, anyway—but my conscience? In what sense, then?

Well, on the other hand, I like gefilte fish; it's never occurred to me to change my last name or to actually deny that I'm Jewish; I've felt the barbs of anti-Semitism on a few occasions in my own life and learned a little—very little, compared to the experience of many others—firsthand of what that's like; and I have to admit to a certain small, private pleasure when I see Jews publicly honored for their accomplishments (a Pulitzer here, a Nobel there). And, of course, some of my best friends are Jews (and though I'd like to think that they'd be my best friends if they were Catholics or Eskimos or Martians, still, I can't help suspecting that their Jewishness just may have a little something to do with it).

Like it or not, as every honest apostate admits—as the old cliché "There's no such thing as an ex-Catholic" acknowledges—there are bonds there. And though like rubber bands they may be stretched pretty far and thin at times, there is some sort of tensile strength that keeps them from breaking, keeps them forever ready to spring back into place with an unexpected snap that often brings me up short, thinking (while I'm wondering whether the bonds that bind can also strangle), So, maybe I'm somehow Jewish after all. Or in spite of it all.

But still, I've gone through most of my life, easily 99 percent of it, without giving it any thought, one way or the other: am I or aren't I? I eat calamari thoughtlessly and with gusto, serve my mother-in-law ham for Christmas dinner, find myself moved by old Protestant hymns, taught for decades at a Presbyterian-affiliated college. I can't speak Yiddish, find the

Hebrew alphabet totally impenetrable, and am given to making snide remarks about Israeli militarism ("killer Jews"), and it never occurs to me to ask other people if they're Jewish . . . or if they're anything. Some of my best friends aren't. And if I'm offended by a crèche on the courthouse lawn, it's not because I think there should be a menorah there too; it's because I believe in the separation of church—any church—and state.

In other words, I think my answer to that query about my identity probably ought to be something like, "Well, you know, not exactly, I'm, like, secular, sort of, and besides, I don't want to be identified with the way a lot of those people have acted, especially with the way they've treated certain others." How's that for ambivalence? "Look at me," I want to say: "*Look* at me! Here: at my face, my flesh. What would you call this in-between, this unsunned tan, color of my skin anyway?" Yes, in midwinter here people regularly ask me where I got my tan. It's just part of the package, I should tell them. Or as I regularly say to my wife in a feeble, comic attempt to define the differences I feel in the white-bread, snow-covered "upper Midwest"—a euphemism for "North"—where I've spent most of my life, "My people are desert people."

Yes, I know, that still makes them "my people." But this oasis of secular ambivalence is where I've generally been setting up my tent all these years, as a reasonably happy if sometimes lonely camper. In a place like this no one needs to pay too much attention to you because you've already located yourself just outside the pale (skins?)—which is (are) always there, the necessary presence for defining, drawing the borders around (the very meaning of the Pale) outsideness.

■

White people: can't live with 'em, can't live without 'em.

The absolutely whitest man I've ever known was a fellow in South India named Kodar, who, with his family, ran a string of what in the old days we would have called general stores. We met the very morning of my arrival in India, where, waiting in the small airport lobby in Cochin for a change of planes, I watched him, a big man in all ways, bob to the surface in a shimmering sea of small black faces like an albino walrus. White hatted, white suited, his face as round and white as the full moon, he came beaming down upon me across that room to introduce himself as the "Head Jew of Cochin" (I could hear the capital letters in his booming voice). Of course, it was in part the contrast with those beautiful and truly black-skinned people of South India that rendered him so startlingly white—though you'd think some of that southern sun would have covered up for the missing pigmentation after all the centuries his family had lived there—but what I was even more startled by was how quickly he'd identified me. Me: nonwhite me! Was I so obvious? Did they know you wherever you were? Glancing down, I realized I was toting an El Al–logoed bag of duty-free scotch, purchased in the Tel Aviv airport where last night's flight to Bombay had originated, but it occurred to me in that same moment that even without this identity badge of booze he'd still have, somehow, known. Like him, this totally white—I mean really white, *white* white!—man, who nonetheless lived in a section of Cochin labeled, as it had been for centuries, Jewtown, my skin (well, maybe my nose too) was the badge of my belonging.

There were (are), as I was eventually to learn there, also black Jews in Cochin—that's what they're called, black Jews—but I was clearly not one of them. I was (if not exactly like Kodar) white. I had arrived, and not just in a foreign country. Well, okay, by my way of seeing things, my particular version of color blindness maybe, white was also a foreign country, and not one to which I'd applied for a visa. Not, for that matter, one I wanted to live in, though sometimes the Indians, too long accustomed to the whiteness of the British Raj, stamped my presence that way too, like a passport of privileges I neither wanted nor deserved. This was not the enclave I'd traveled halfway around the world to live in. What was happening, I could see, was that, just as it had happened when I entered the business world, I was being handed one of those white shirts and told which side I was on in a game I didn't even want to play.

These were nice people, the Kodars, don't mistake me, and as I was also to learn, they sure knew how to throw a party (a very Indian, very Jewish party: fish curry and sauteed chili peppers at a Simchas Torah feast), but their generosity did not do a lot for my comfort level. Just as they were ready to sweep me up in the arms of their ethnicity (didn't I know some nice Jewish girls their sons could marry?), so they pulled me into the cage of whiteness they dwelt in, where they were well served, as they had been for centuries, much like the imperial Brits, by the black Jews who labored in their shops, cleaned their homes, and weren't allowed to sit in their synagogue or marry their daughters. This seemed all too familiar to me. And there I was opting out all over again.

But parting is never easy. On the way out of the wine business and off to graduate school, my father, more sympathetic than I'd expected, and probably long since aware of my misfit status there, generously decided to keep me on the payroll (at a greatly reduced level, needless to say) and the Blue Cross plan for a while, making my finances for the next couple of years considerably easier than they would have been otherwise. Oh, I lived with my young family (could it, I wonder now, have been his grandchildren he was most concerned about?) in the same tacky married-student housing as everyone else, with the balky oil heater sitting in the center of the living room and the Pacific Northwest's famous green mold creeping up the walls, and ate the same endless spaghetti dinners. But unlike my peers (or so I imagined; maybe they all had private incomes—it wasn't something we talked about), I never suffered anxiety about whether I'd be able to pay the kids' doctor bills or the rent at the end of the month.

With my nose to the academic grindstone all day and much of the night—I did have a future to be anxious about, with three little mouths to feed—what I wholly managed to avoid thinking about was where that money that was making my life a little easier was coming from. Which was, of course, the same place as before. I thought I was happily working on a Ph.D. in English, whereas, in a very real sense—though practiced as I was, I managed to go a long time not thinking about it at all—I was right back in the winery, with only the intriguing aroma of my dissertation and the far more powerful stench of dirty diapers to block out that winey smell wafting bitterly west against both the prevailing winds and the flimsy naïveté of my ethics.

■

Meanwhile, back at the winery (or, rather, back in my days at the winery), ever the young liberal, I had once challenged my father, when we had one of our infrequent job openings, as to why we didn't have any blacks—I suppose I must have said Negroes back then—working in the plant. His reply wasn't the overtly racist one I might have expected—they're lazy, undependable, you can't trust them . . . the sort of thing I heard often enough from his country club friends—but the practical businessman's response: all his other workers would quit.

He may well have been right. His other workers I knew well from having worked summers with them during college on the bottling line and loading dock. They drove hours to and from the plant in their beat-up Fords from their Appalachian-foothill farms where they'd been out working their tobacco patches at dawn and would be back working them again from the time they got home till sundown. They were lean, muscled, hardworking, underpaid men, barely literate for the most part, who spoke a version of English so strange to me that talking with them was like learning a foreign language, and I often had to ask them to repeat themselves two or three times before I understood what they were saying.

"Set them bottles rat cheer," Nolly Goldsberry might say to me.

And eventually I learned to put those bottles right here.

But however foreign they might have seemed, they were—and they knew they were—white men. They didn't have much—rusty, old cars; low-paying jobs; tiny, unproductive patches of land—but they had that and they had their pride, and, as they made clear to me in the midsummer northern Kentucky heat of our windowless lunchroom, between coarse jokes and arcane tobacco talk and occasional sessions of fiddle playing, they weren't about to let some "nigger" take away any of what little they had.

They weren't the Jews I was beginning to fret about, who had long since removed themselves from the pushcarts and sweatshops of their immigrant past, but they could have been. At the bottom of the socioeconomic ladder, an alienated, isolated people who struggled to survive well outside the prosperous suburbs of flourishing post–World War II America, they still managed to define themselves in a way that allied them with white America and clearly differentiated them from those others, those darker-skinned people they weren't about to let get so much as a foot on the ladder if they could help it.

And my father, like most of his contemporaries, took their side. They were, after all, white people. Just like Jews.

White people: what choice was there but to opt out when

they were beginning to make me feel like they were tightening a metaphorical noose around my own neck?

And it's still there after a fashion, though it looks more like a tie right now, a very elegant Italian-silk tie, in fact, that's in no danger of strangling me but serves as a nice metaphorical reminder that I'm still struggling with knots. It goes well with the suit I'm wearing, which in turn seems to fit nicely with the car I'm driving, a new silver Saab, which might be fast enough to make a good getaway car but instead is only another reminder that for all my opting out, I haven't actually gotten very far from the winery in spite of how many decades have passed since I last hoisted a case of muscatel onto the back of a semi or how far afield I've moved both professionally and geographically.

I turned down the wine-colored leather seats for charcoal: a decision, my psychoanalyst might say if I had one, not without a certain symbolic value, because were it not for the winery and my lifelong struggle to leave behind what it had come to represent for me, I wouldn't be driving this car. I wouldn't be without wheels—I've been able to make my own way in the world reasonably well all these years, thank you—but they wouldn't be *these* expensive wheels. These are the wheels my father willed me, so to speak. When he sold the wine company and retired, he found himself reasonably well off but with a bundle of money to invest and a desire to stay at least somewhat active in the business world. That money that took good care of me as a kid, that sent me off to college and bought me, yes, even my first (far less stylish) car, when I graduated. That would see him through the rest of his life in the comfortable style to which he had become accustomed. That money that, invested at one time in a chain of coin laundromats, finally in commercial real estate, would eventually come down, in this odd automotive way, to my brother and myself.

Laundered money, I can't help thinking, recalling accompanying him on some of his coin-collecting rounds when I paid my regular visits back to town. However far removed from its making, there's still the implication that it was dirty money to begin with, not criminal but ethically questionable cash, which there really hasn't seemed much point in turning down at this late date. But that takes me right back to where I began both my adult life and this essay. Here I am, even after all these years, standing in front of the mirror, buttoning my nice cotton shirt, tightening my tie, and wrestling with the angel of my conscience—or is it the demon of my identity?—who still has a stranglehold on me.

# SLOW LEARNERS

It's nearly as hard to imagine as a visit to another planet: I'm in the Bond Hill Theater, where in 1942 and '43 I used to get in for free on Saturdays instead of for a dime if I brought a little-red-wagon load of scrap metal, coat hangers, and stuff— who knew what most of it was?—that I'd picked up alongside the railroad tracks half a mile from home. We cheered when the newsreels came on showing Zeros and Messerschmitts being blasted from the sky, plunging earthward in smoky spirals. We hissed when the sing-along short appeared, asking us to follow the little bouncing ball, but we sang along anyway. We cheered for the cartoon and even more so for the next installment of the weekly serial, which relieved at last the tension of last week's ending, when the stagecoach with the heroine aboard had gone off the cliff after the driver had been shot by the villain. But now we cheered when we saw how the hero had leaped aboard at the last moment and pulled her off, so that they went rolling in the sagebrush and were not in the coach as it crashed down the cliff and broke into hundreds of deadly pieces. And we cheered even louder when the feature came on, though we were just as quick to groan with dismay when Gene Autry tuned up his guitar and began to sing beside the campfire. It was wartime, and we hadn't come for the singing, as all of you from my generation know perfectly well.

Now it's fifteen years later, and the theater is no longer a theater but the site of an ongoing revival meeting, and instead of sitting in my sticky leatherette seat with an equally sticky handful of malted milk balls, watching the dependable good guys in white hats saying the predictable things about how they are going to take care of the bad guys in the black hats in order to restore the rule of law and order, I am standing at the very back, behind a tarnished brass railing, hearing language I have never heard before: unpredictable, lawless, disordered, indecipherable. They don't show movies here at the Bond Hill Theater anymore; they hold meetings every Wednesday, Friday, and Sunday night instead, led by a dynamic black preacher, and the people we are watching on this particular Friday night are, I have been led to understand, doing something called speaking in tongues. For me, at least, the times have changed.

The primary difference is that now I am a tourist here. Now I am not part of a cheering or hissing crowd. The people around me now are not the other kids from Fenmore Drive and environs who have hauled their own loads of rusting scrap metal over the sidewalks and down the bumpy curbs and across wide streets, which gas rationing has rendered relatively free of traffic, for a cheap afternoon's entertainment in support of the war effort but a handful of young marrieds like myself, come to see . . . what? It is, in a way—and yes, I know I have taken a long, slow time to come around to this—my first conscious acknowledgment that there is another world out there.

Of course, I'd been through everything the educational system had to offer on the subject: the American Indians in grade school, the Jukes and the Kallikaks in high school, the Trobriand Islanders in college (with the Elizabethans yet to come in graduate school). This was very much premulticultural, understand, from those benighted if less confusing days before we began to learn that everybody is the same as us only different. I got pretty good grades, too, presumably indicative of the fact that I understood what I was expected to understand about those various people. And I suppose I did, but the problem was that I understood them in exactly the same way that I understood algebra and the First Constitutional Convention and *Ivanhoe*—which is to say, I understood them in the way they were given to me to understand, as objects of study, not as the people they were or had been, in all their amazing otherness.

The Jukes and the Kallikaks (to take an example that I suspect you had to be there to appreciate), those appalling and wonderful and—as we learned much later—wholly fictitious Appalachian models of the dissolute and the ordinary, were nothing more than an object lesson in Mendelian genetics, as much like every other such lesson we got as, well, peas in a pod. (Needless to say, the built-in and heavily emphasized moral lesson on the merits of exogamy was not lost on us; we weren't that slow, at least on a topic such as sex that we had some personal interest in.) The Trobrianders, likewise, were merely models of anthropological methodology; for all we knew—and for all it mattered in that particular context— they too might just as well have been made up. As for the Indians, western mythologizing had already pretty well completed the task of fictionalizing and objectifying them; there wasn't much happening at school to contradict what we saw on the screen on Saturday. And the Elizabethans, in those innocent, precontextualizing days of my graduate career, would be reduced to little more than "background."

It was in Sunday school, of all places, that I had the first real lesson in genuine otherness pounded into me, one that, had I been less a slow learner, should have dramatically alerted me to the possibilities of what was out there. And this came not from my introduction to Pharaoh's minions or the ancient Israelites, but thanks to crazy Kenny—which is still, after all these years and his sad end, the only way I can think about him—who one Sunday morning leaped upon me from behind as we were descending the stairwell immediately after class and drove me down on the linoleum landing and started punching me in the face until . . . But wait: let's go back a bit.

We're in class still. Our teacher, the rabbi's son, is lecturing this enforced gathering of sleepy ten or eleven year olds about . . . who knows, whatever rabbis' sons lecture about. It doesn't matter; no one is paying attention anyway. Kenny, out of my line of vision a couple of rows back and a row or two over, has just lofted a paper airplane into this solemn atmosphere thickened by boredom and a general desire to be elsewhere. Sunday-morning slothfulness has turned us into flies already submerged in the gummy sap that will soon harden into the amber petrification of the rest of our lives. Above this lifeless desert Kenny's paper airplane soars for a moment—stays aloft a little longer than any of the rabbi's son's weighty words—then glides to a landing in the aisle, more or less at my feet. It's the nature of flight as I've observed it: you go up a little ways, then you come down. So I pay no more attention to it than to look around to see where it's come from—mere curiosity: wherever it came from has to be more interesting than whatever place the rabbi's son is lecturing from.

It's then that I see Kenny gesticulating at me. Under his thick, curly red hair he is scrunching up his eyes, mouthing things, even waving his arms in a kind of sticky slow motion. What is he trying to say? Send my paper airplane back? Maybe. But is that my responsibility? It's only a lousy piece of scribbled-on, folded-up paper. Why should I bother? It takes such an effort to make any sort of move in the heavy syrup of Sunday morning congealing about us. Besides, the rabbi's son has suddenly begun to sound so earnest—he is passionately appealing to us now to contribute a portion of our weekly allowances to the planting of trees in the deserts of Palestine—

and Kenny is so inarticulate, a blurry conglomeration of extravagant gestures and ugly grimaces, that I turn away and ignore his appeal, if that is what it is, as, finally, I will also ignore the rabbi's son's appeals. They have nothing to do with me. They come from other worlds, in languages I have not, to my ultimately bloody-nosed dismay, yet learned to understand.

Whatever lesson Kenny thinks, a few minutes later, that he is pounding into me on the stairwell landing—that he is bigger and stronger and righter and angrier and I am a little weasel—it is not, I eventually come to believe, however accurate, the lesson I should have been learning then.

Philosophers have long wearied this issue of other minds—their knowability (or not). Psychologists likewise, from their own various perspectives, theoretical or experimental, have struggled to gain some understanding of this same issue, sometimes, in their frustration, even finding it necessary to deny the mind's very existence. Anthropologists have extended the concern to whole cultures, and so have science fiction writers, though for the most part the ideas the latter have about the workings of other cultures, other minds, merely duplicate in reductive fashion what little we know of our own minds and cultures. But you don't have to travel to distant galaxies or gain the intellectual expertise of one of the aforementioned disciplines to engage with other worlds. As I had only just begun to perceive while sitting woozily on a cold, hard stair holding a blood-soaked handkerchief to my nose, and as I finally had to acknowledge while clinging to the railing at the rear of the former Bond Hill Theater as people flailing in the aisles cried out helplessly in remarkable and indecipherable voices, they are around us everywhere.

The black maid Rosa Thomas, who started coming to us once
a week when we moved to the big, new house on Westminster
Drive, arrived from a world whose existence I certainly was,
intellectually at least, aware of: the West End ghetto. But it
had no real existence for me, nor, I think, did she once she left
our house at the end of the day. When she was there she was
very much there—small and muscular, hardworking, sometimes startlingly witty: not other, but simply a person going
about her regular duties in a wholly comprehensible way, not
unlike my mother preparing dinner—but once she was gone,
though she had bused away to a world wholly other than the
one I knew and shared with her once a week, rather than becoming the other that I might have wondered about, she simply became . . . not. It was, no doubt, the easiest way for me
to deal with my ignorance. I might have said the same about
my girlfriend of the time. The world of her Orthodox home,
the world of poor Jews of whom I had heard only vague ru-
mors, differed vastly from my own secular, middle-class
world, almost as much so as another country, they did things
so differently there. But inasmuch as I was rarely admitted beyond the front door of her family's small apartment, its existence was always somehow less than real, and so unlike the
dense intensity, the simple physicality, of her presence with
me that it was almost as if it didn't exist: she was a Cinderella
who came from and then, at evening's end, disappeared back
into a bleak and other world of which I was to know nothing.
As I suspect she would have been the first to attest—because I
was no Prince Charming and what, finally, did I really even
know about her?—I was a slow learner indeed.

Orthodoxies baffle me no end. I say this not to condemn those who hold orthodox beliefs—though in fact I have little sympathy with them (their beliefs, that is, not the individuals)—but to acknowledge a whole and quite enormous category of otherness that I simply do not comprehend. Call it my failing, another example of how slow I can be at grasping certain powerful forces that are alien to me even at this late point in my life. Or call it my heritage, handed down to me from a father whose rejection of the demands of orthodoxy earned my sympathy, altered my life, and left me puzzling over the power of orthodoxy forever after. But it's not because I'm incapable of understanding the whatness of orthodoxy: its rules and rituals, its shalls and shall nots, its texts and contexts. My problem is with how, not what: How do people—how does the human mind, the most remarkable and flexible organ of adaptation that the whole Darwinian history of development has produced so far, the current end point of all that consciousness has become capable of—buy into that stuff? By what otherworldly process do otherwise sane, intelligent, and self-determining members of my species surrender thought to thoughtlessness and commit themselves to arcane and inexplicable and (in the age of Jonestown and Waco and Heaven's Gate) sometimes downright deadly rituals, to theories that don't even seem embarrassed to contradict both good sense and all available evidence, to the claimed divinity of arbitrary hierarchies and the all too often horrifying abuse of others? The muddling of thought by passion, even its sometime total submergence under the tides of the emotions, I can understand, having, like most of us, been so inundated from time to time. But orthodoxy is just the opposite of passion: it is a choice—something the emotions don't give us—and a lifelong commitment. And in its rigidity—the single quality aside from its presumed rightness that it tends to be most proud of—it does not admit of possibility. The final truths it proposes, as the philosopher

Isaiah Berlin has pointed out in *The Sense of Reality,* all too readily clear the path for final solutions.

■

I have of late been in dispute with a neighbor regarding property lines. We live part-time in the country—in the wilderness, to be precise—far from the right-angled platting of rectangular city lots. Here there are few fences, and the balsams and birches, as well as the deer and wolves and black bears, and the meandering little creeks, make their way indiscriminately across invisible borders. No one cares. Hardly anyone around here even posts their land against hunting or trespassing, and more than once I have found myself chatting with strangers who have wandered up my path from the beach. My path because I made it (and repair it annually), but not, please note, *my* beach: though I pay higher taxes for my meager frontage on Lake Superior, all of the shore up to the vegetation line is public property, theirs for the enjoyment I'm happy to see them take advantage of. Let them collect all the agates they want; next year the lake will put more back.

But I, it appears, am the snake in this woodland idyll.

Let me, again, back up a bit. When I first, and finally, began to build on these two and a half acres, my neighbor— we'll call him X, because it's the unknown other we're talking about here—came rushing over, at a time when I wasn't around, and brought the digging of the septic field to a halt with the claim that it was intruding on his property. Upon my return the following week, I went over to talk to him, proposing that we split the cost of a survey to confirm the boundary, but he, much to my relief, told me that wasn't necessary and apologized for his hasty overreaction. I presumed that because the land had been vacant for so many years, he must have felt that any construction was an intrusion on his world, and I was glad to see things so easily resolved. And so we became, over

the years, if not exactly friends—our houses are only barely
visible to each other—then okay neighbors. One frigid winter
day when my car wouldn't start he gave me a tow, another
time he came over in my absence and planted some rhubarb in
the yard, and I have sent countless customers (myself in-
cluded) to the ever-expanding gift shop that occupies most of
his house and several outbuildings.

A lengthy introduction, but here's the heart of the matter:
the little sauna that my contractor built for me the summer
we finished the house—a baby dome that mimics the geodesic
dome we live in here—sits, it now turns out subsequent to a
survey that X has just had done (he's considering selling his
property), on my neighbor's property. Just barely, but, still,
that appears to be the fact of it. It occupies all of about 150
square feet of his 7.6 acres, about the size of an ordinary bedroom and well away from his house, the highway, or any otherwise usable land, on the soft till above a runoff creek. No
kidding, I actually did this: unknowingly, unintentionally,
unaware that this was not part of my own land, I built a sauna.
And in that little hemisphere of ignorance I have been happily
sweating away my aches and pains these past sixteen years.
But however inadvertently, I am clearly in the wrong here.
The question, though—the question that remains to us now,
post facto, as human beings, not as legal entities—is: what do
we do about it?

And the ire (X's) and irony (mine) of it is that although I
have perhaps broken the law—"flagrantly," to hear X tell it
(but if so flagrant, why didn't he object the moment construction began?)—the law is now on my side. The evening of the
very day the survey was completed he was at my door demanding that the sauna be removed at once. Belligerent even:
no other options. I appealed on various grounds, not the least
being what seems to me the humane quality of neighborliness
as well as the incidental impact, if any, that this little building

had on his vast landholdings. Nothing doing. I offered to purchase that little square of earth from him, or a larger slice if he so preferred, for whatever he might deem a reasonable price. Nothing doing there, either, though this was the point at which the oddest orthodoxy I'd yet heard of put in its rigid appearance.

No, he couldn't part with any part of that in any fashion because from the marker on the highway to a post the surveyor had set up farther back in the woods was a straight line, and the straight line was—his own word, I swear it—"sacred." Never mind that it took a sharp turn southwest at that post and a whole series of other jagged turns before it ended up back at the highway on the far side of his fiefdom: this straight line was "sacred."

It is, I believe, a basic principle of orthodoxy that anything—any act or object—can be made sacred simply by the decree of the high priest, the waving of a wand of magical words or an appropriate convening of, say, the elders. X is the high priest and prophet of his property, and his ruling is beyond appeal. One is perhaps reminded just a bit of the recent bloody squabble between Jews and Muslims at the Temple Mount (whoops, Haram al-Sharif: I want to be sure to tread on everybody's orthodoxies equally). Though we have yet to go that far here, the anger of the orthodox is not to be taken lightly once its sacred grounds have been trampled on.

And trample, I must confess, I have done: not just in my original faux pas of building where I did (and where I certainly would not had I known), but by informing him, lately, of the legal concept of adverse possession (which maybe you know less technically as "squatter's rights"), by which use of land without objection for a period of fifteen years grants ownership. Well, sixteen years have passed. X has never before objected to this little, round twelve-foot-diameter building. And in fact I don't even want possession of that little chunk of land. Ownership holds no appeal for me. Don't even get me started on private property. An easement—the simple right to keep on steaming my bones over there—will do just fine, and I'll even pay for the privilege.

But even so it is, apparently (mentally, at least, for an easement would not in legal fact adjust the property line or affect the sale of the property), an intrusion on the sacred straight line. And—this is where I really don't get it, where orthodoxy becomes wholly other to me in a deeply personal way—the arbitrarily defined sacredness of the object takes precedence over the qualities I would like to think we are capable of: neighborliness, friendship, compassion, generosity, understanding, forgiveness. In the name of spirituality more often than not ("My gut feeling" is X's secular version), in the orthodox belief in rightness, in unshakable flat-earthness and the certainty that not just the moon but also the planets, sun, and stars all revolve around us—I'm reminded of Frost's neighbor in "Mending Wall":

> . . . like an old-stone savage armed.
> He moves in darkness as it seems to me,
> Not of woods only and the shade of trees.
> He will not go behind his father's saying,
> And he likes having thought of it so well
> He says again, "Good fences make good neighbors."

—the human spirit gets shut down. Perhaps what I'm slowest of all at comprehending is that there are human mind-sets so alien to me that though I have no choice but to acknowledge their existence, I will never truly understand them.

So be it, I suppose you could say. Who says you need to get a handle on all this otherness? Life is filled with encounters, many of them as unpredictable and potentially unpleasant as meeting up with one of the bears who populate your wilderness could be, who just like these people act and articulate in ways you will never be able to understand. Why should you expend your own best resources banging your head against the impermeable wall of their otherness? Chances are that if you did break through, you wouldn't much like what you found. When, in book 2, canto 12, of *The Faerie Queene,* Spenser's knight, Guyon, finally leaves the Bowre of Blisse, and Grill, one of the men whom he has rescued from the animal forms into which the enchantress has transformed them, chooses to remain behind in the shape of a pig, there's nothing for Guyon to do but throw up his hands in despair: "Let Grill be Grill, and have his hoggish mind." What else can he do? One of the things you slow learners trying late in life to catch up on everything you think you need to know need to learn is that you don't need to learn it all. Slow down.

Well, gee, thanks for the lecture, the moral uplift there, the attempt to make me feel better about my inadequacies, but, you know, it isn't all that easy for some of us. Lacking the papier-mâché bedrock of orthodoxy to pillow our heads on, life tends to be something of a puzzle—an interesting puzzle, let me add—and the nature of the other is an intriguing and important piece of that puzzle. Without the other, after all, with all its opacity and sometimes even belligerence, what would we all be but pretty much the same, a veritable orthodoxy of identity as it were, sworn to serve as Odysseus's loyal and single-minded crew—Circe's island being the source for Spenser's Bowre of Blisse—on whatever zany, lifelong voyage he takes us, no matter how much we'd rather be sleeping in our own beds or even, like our porcine friend, giving up this tourist life to settle down on one of those marvelous islands we've never seen before, enchanted by the possibilities of otherness?

Not many months after watching, struck silent myself, the re-
vivalist inspiration that bubbled forth in an utter otherness of
language from those leaping, babbling strangers in the former
Bond Hill Theater, I attended Calvary Baptist Church one
evening—in Rosa Thomas's neighborhood this time, not my
own—to hear Mahalia Jackson sing. I was, again, a tourist,
standing off to the side of this enormous chamber in much the
same small group as before, certainly not a worshiper, but
caught up, this time, as I never was by that preacher, in this
woman's huge and amazing voice. But not, I soon saw, like others were, who burst suddenly not into song but into speaking
in tongues. They rose in the pews and threw their arms in the
air as if grasping for some treasure just beyond their reach, and
if anyone knew what they were saying, it certainly wasn't I.
They fell to the floor in the stony aisles, some of them, spinning as they spoke, their speech as dizzying as the whirl of
their bodies. And Mahalia Jackson sang on, transporting them
into this otherness that I only much later realized they must
have long sought: an otherness that sailed them away from the
shores of their daily lives and gave them a vision of what else
might lie out there on the distant seas of possibility. I can see
now what that sense of being transported is all about, how
they were, for this time—and who knew how long afterward—changed, and this much I can understand, even if I
don't have a clue about how or into what.

There is another world out there, indeed, and what I can see
now—slow is not forever—is that it teems with possibility. It
is a vast sea dotted with islands, archipelagoes, Australia-size
continents of possibility, and if some of them are dry and in-
hospitable, where you would have to scratch the brutal and
unforgiving soil for a living and pray for rescue, others are as
lush with possibility as . . . as . . . the human mind itself, that
forested tangle of greenery inside whose dense and immeasur-
able branchings countless unseen denizens are chattering and

singing and growling and mumbling, a ripening of voices only a few of which we can, at any one time, disentangle to meet our own needs.

Because yes, the other is inside us as well.

When, a couple of decades after that bloody Sunday morning of distant memory, I heard that Kenny had killed himself, I was, though not surprised at the news itself, surprised by the sudden sadness that news left me feeling. I hardly knew him, after all. I had little direct contact with him after that one incident and no recollection of his presence in any further part of my slow climb up the teenage slope toward the plateau of adulthood. I wouldn't have known the man he'd become if I'd seen him on the streets, and, besides, I'd long since left those streets themselves behind as I'd moved on—and off—in my own life. It was on a visit back sometime in my thirties that a cousin informed me of his death. Though typically for me, forever trying to get a grasp on my feelings, I didn't much respond at the time, what I discovered afterward was one of those strange, hollow feelings we sometimes get, a little echo chamber in the center of the self, a space carved out in which to put away something that was, suddenly, no longer there.

It's taken me till now, slow learner still, to realize that in some odd way I'd carried Kenny with me all those years. Wholly baffled as I'd been back then by what kind of person would do what he had done on such slight and mostly imagined provocation, I had taken some piece of his inexplicable otherness, which so mystified me that I couldn't let go of it, and encapsulated it solidly in myself. And there it had lain all those years, no doubt only one among countless little time capsules of my youth, just waiting for the proper signal to reopen it.

Only to find nothing there, like cracking open an egg to find someone had already sucked its innards out. Because that, after all, is what the other is to us: an emptiness. We can fill it with what we want—luminous oneness with the universe, solar flares of rage, landfills of urban detritus—but that's us, not it, our fears or imaginings. The other is other, is absence, and in the impossible struggle to know it, we take it inside ourselves and so make even ourselves, in some way, other— even to ourselves. If I know myself more as a result of this process, it's because, in an almost literal way, I have taken crazy Kenny to heart. I have lived with his otherness. I make no claim to understanding it; his version of speaking in tongues was addressing my face with his fists. But its presence is palpable, a part of me, as are those others whose voices were raised up to a pitch beyond my hearing. If it takes a whole life to learn to live with them, to accept the extent to which we carry within us vast pockets of ignorance, so be it. That may even give me time enough to invite my aggrieved neighbor, X, and his passion for the sacred straight line into this con- glomerate I think of as myself (much as I may doubt his desire or ability to reciprocate), along with a couple of strangely scrambled colleagues I know I'll also never be able to under- stand.

Understanding isn't everything.

□

# PAUSE A WHILE

The dead should just shut up.
—Ellen Bryant Voigt, "Ravenous"

A dear friend of mine who also hangs out in northern Minnesota wears with considerable delight his new sweatshirt, a gift from his wife, displaying on his chest, on an outline map of Lake Superior, the names of all the ships that have sunk there, a tiny outline drawing of each ship positioned on the map at the spot where it went down, with the date of its sinking duly noted. It's a very cool sweatshirt, and sometimes, in spite of a family tradition of avoiding cemeteries, I find myself thinking I'd like one just like it, and the book that's available to accompany it as well, *Lake Superior: Graveyard of Ships,* to fill in those outlines. But no, I've seen enough of graveyards. I don't really want to be a walking display of one of the biggest—certainly in area—and most brutal of them, where death and burial occur simultaneously.

This one, in particular, gets romanticized these days, when improvements in navigation and weather forecasting and marine safety have rendered the shipping lanes safer than ever. Radar, loran, and global-positioning satellites have helped to pacify even this notorious killer of a lake, and technological innovations have reduced crew sizes to numbers that corporate ship owners and their insurers doubtless register in the range of "acceptable losses." Automated beacons have replaced the old lighthouses; the famous Split Rock Lighthouse on Minnesota's north shore has outlived its nautical usefulness and gone into an even more active old age as a state park and history center, a monument to the Days When, complete with a gift shop offering tourists those reminders of its grim past.

The lakers and salties, as they're called here, the big ore boats three football fields long headed for the steel mills on the eastern Great Lakes and the foreign cargo ships that sail up through the St. Lawrence Seaway for grain, traverse Superior in relative safety now. Though a fierce gale dragged the Panamanian saltie *Seadaniel* ashore, anchors and all, in Duluth in November 1996, there was no loss of life, and the event became, as such things do these days, not a tragedy but a tourist attraction. The last big ship to go down was the *Edmund Fitzgerald,* caught in a fierce November storm in 1975 en route to Detroit with a load of iron-ore pellets, its crew of twenty-nine still entombed a quarter century later under a thousand feet of icy water but its disaster lifted out of reality and into the realm of legend by Gordon Lightfoot's ballad. Should you be in a mood for this strange sense of nostalgia, this deification of the deadly, its ship's bell, recovered in 1995 and restored, is now on permanent display at the Great Lakes Shipwreck Museum on Whitefish Point on Michigan's Upper Peninsula.

But I don't buy the romance of death by drowning or—more commonly these days when the victims tend to be foolhardy fishermen and even more foolish drunken boaters (or a combination thereof)—by hypothermia: forty-degree waters don't give you much time to repent your beers, your sins, or your errors of judgment. I don't buy the romance of death, period. I can stand on my little pebbled beach here on the north shore and sense both the beauty and the menace of this greatest of the Great Lakes, but there's nothing romantic about the latter. Easy as it might be here at water's edge to look out over this inland sea as if it were an enormous graveyard stretching to the far horizon and listen to the waves sliding over the gravel as if they were whispering what the lake held in its depths, I don't smell death in the wind when it swings around to the east and picks up an icy edge as it comes scurrying across these frigid waters. A cold wind is just a cold wind, chilling me right through all the layers I've wrapped myself up in and sending me scurrying back to the house.

But even when I set my back to it to climb the path uphill and away, I can still hear that gravelly voice growling behind me. One of those old tacit family mottos—Let the Dead Bury the Dead—is pulling me home, but like Orpheus checking to make sure that all that's been lost is still really there, I can't help turning back for one more look, one more listen.

My mother's grave, I was surprised to learn, is in the same cemetery as my great-grandfather's, which I also didn't know about, thanks to a family that buried him deeper than any grave digger ever thought of doing. Out of Sight, Out of Mind must have been another of those family mottos once they'd slid David Greenberg into the ground. By the time I was trying to metaphorically dig him up eighty years later, not only did no one remember where they'd put him, but they didn't even remember that he'd existed. Hamilton County's Vital Records Office did, however, and even though the name of the "place of burial" listed on the death certificate they'd provided me with had changed, and the successor to the funeral home also listed there had no record of him, I'd done my detective work. And so I conned my brother, my younger son, and his wife and their young son into accompanying me on a bitter-cold Cincinnati January morning, with an appropriately bone-chilling wind swirling among the stones of that little hilltop Hirsch Hoffert Cemetery, to see what we could find.

One of the things I found while wandering around on my own there was a little poem, inscribed on one face of an impressive obelisk of a monument:

> Pause a while
> As you pass by.
> As you are now
> So once was I.
>
> As I am now
> So you will be.
> Prepare for death
> And follow me.

A colleague tells me that this is a common inscription in English graveyards, but never having encountered it before, and standing around that January in that icy wind whipping among the stones, frustrated at not yet having found the object of my search, I paused for a shivering moment to commit it to memory, acknowledging as I did so that the dead clearly do not follow our instructions: they will not "just shut up."

In spite of its initial reluctance, this particular cemetery had a lot to say.

By the time I rejoined the others, that damp and frigid wind had finally gotten the better of everyone, and a wise consensus had been rapidly reached to abandon the search and head back to the warmth of the car. We were standing at the edge of the cemetery by then, little Max wrapped in his father's arms for warmth, the five of us poised on the slight rise above the tiny parking lot, when I turned for one last look. No one was there besides our small group, no one else foolish enough to be out there on a wind-swept hilltop on such a morning, and no sound to be heard aside from that wind in the bare oak trees and my brother's voice urging immediate departure. All the help I'd been given for finding the grave, from the County Records Office and the Weil Funeral Home and one Dorothy Shostle, secretary of the cemetery association, had been no help at all. Even the most apparently precise directions I'd finally received for locating the graves of David Greenberg and his wife, Minnie—line G, lots 23 and 24—had proved useless where there were no line or lot numbers to be found and all the alphabetizing and counting we'd done had added up to nothing.

And then I spotted it, just two rows in. Not his, but hers: Minnie Greenberg, March 16, 1855, to March 15, 1934. And there, next to it, the simple stone reading DAVID GREENBERG, January 9, 1853, to June 23, 1917, and then, in large capital letters below that, POET. And a line of Hebrew letters above his name in which I recognized the words *Ben Yishai,* the pen name he used for his poetry.

For both of them, curiously, the dates differed slightly from what I'd learned before. In the 1900 U.S. Census I'd found Minnie's birth date listed as in January, David's as in December of the preceding year; the death certificate, on the other hand, listed his birth date as "Feb?" and the date of his death as June 22; and the obituaries I'd read also listed his death date as June 22. Who can you believe? Does the grave marker get the final word? One way or another, it would seem, the conversation with the dead goes on.

Meanwhile, in spite of the way the others were whistling me back to the car as if I were a good dog, I stayed to photograph both headstones. I wasn't even feeling the cold any longer. I was satisfied just to stand there for a few minutes, to know that harsh as the day was, I'd finally found everything I'd come for.

But I was wrong.

■

I have seen the eloquent acres of Arlington and the sea-level cemeteries of New Orleans, where the dead float on the surface in their marble boats. I have wandered through Feist Pet Cemetery, where fat gray squirrels scrambled over headstones that wept for little dogs lost, and I have fished the Sawmill Creek along the edge of Crystal Bay Cemetery and caught, as usual, nothing. Like an icon of the quick and the dead, I have done my daily runs through the cemeteries of suburban St. Paul, wondering as I leaped over markers set flush in the ground what those below—or their loved ones above—would have to say about my passage, a thought that hastened my pace, especially when I spotted a group of people convening for their grim task or a long line of dark cars circling my way. I have stood sweating in the summer sun in Cincinnati's Walnut Hills Cemetery, listening to the evocative silence of my father and his family, much as it was in life. And in the Woodbury United Methodist Cemetery I have knelt in the grass before Wendy Parrish's headstone, hearing her own voice in the words from her poem "Melody in Burghley Field" inscribed on it:

> oh I have left my home
> and all my companions are sleepers
> and the quiet of the ladybug and the white clouds

And I have known how the poem then followed to its end:

> oh I was mostly raised
> and am now down deep in the field
> oh and I have dropped out of sight.

But not, I always add to myself, out of hearing.

When I visited my friends the Watsons in Los Angeles many years ago, they considered a trip to Forest Lawn mandatory, a quirky notion of tourism, in my experience, that I at first discounted on the basis of their being not only Californians but also recently transplanted Canadians—until I found myself so intrigued by this Disneyland of death that they finally had to come searching for me where I was wandering through a chorus of chubby cherubs in the children's grove in order to drag me back to the land of the living. I'd long since lost track of time rambling through the Vale of Morning Light, the Glade of Loving Kindness, the Columbarium of Radiant Light, and the Court of Remembrance, so the Watsons must have imagined I'd passed through the waters of Lethe by then, but it's an experience I've never been able to forget, no more than Evelyn Waugh could, who turned his response to it into his novel *The Loved One:* his vision of death American style as kitsch.

I didn't know what it was for me then, but I think I've begun to learn since. Funerary practices tell us a lot not only about cultures—a subject much written about—but also about who we are as individuals, as families. I was deeply touched when, a few years ago, I accompanied my wife on a pilgrimage to her father's hometown of Milton, Wisconsin, and was privileged to watch her, from a little park across the street where I was minding our three dogs, as she wandered through the small cemetery there and knelt before her father's grave. And Wendy's parents faithfully tend the roses they planted beside her headstone those many years ago. Cemeteries are places for the living to come—as in most cases they will eventually do anyway—with their memories intact and their senses attuned to what that populous world has to say to them.

But in my family, though I've never heard anyone refer to it as the ghoulish practice I know some others think it is, we have never been great visitors of the dead. Though he must have known it was a common practice, it seems never to have occurred to my father to visit the graves of his parents or that of either his first or second wife. On only one occasion was I able to talk him into going to the cemetery where he himself resides now, in the midst of his family, but the only thing he was interested in was searching for his former business partner's grave. We never did find it. The idea of visiting a famous cemetery or the graveyard of a famous individual, to say nothing of the places where his loved ones, including my mother, were interred, seems to have been as remote to him as a journey to Mars. My brother, in recent years, has begun to pay the traditional Memorial Day floral visit to the parental plot, but I suspect this has far more to do with the onset of the sentimentality of advancing age, the crux of conscience and chronology, than with any deep-rooted familial practice. My ex-wife leaves town the instant anyone close to her dies. And we're not alone, of course: my friend Juanita Garciagodoy reports in her book *Digging the Days of the Dead,* a book that is all about celebrations of cemeteries and visits to the beloved dead, that "I have never visited the grave or cremation urn of a dead relative, nor have I been invited to do so by any family member; . . . I do not even know if anyone pays such visits." And I myself am prone to slipping away as soon as the funeral services are over, reluctant to attach my own car to that long, slow line grimly wending its way to the cemetery behind the solitary motorcycle cop.

Still, the graveyard exerts its pull on me: a mutual attraction, I suppose, the way we're drawn to water or love, and consistent with the understanding I've come to have of myself as someone who's not much good at letting go, who continues to want (and under certain circumstances to seek out) the cool of polished granite, the shade of the overhanging oak, the smell of roses and whisper of wind—whatever form of contact such places, such visits, might provide.

It was a considerably more pleasant season—late June, the sun in the early evening still well up above the horizon, Ohio Valley humidity sliding up from the river bottom on a light breeze to ease over us like a damp cloth moistening the late heat of the day—when I returned to Hirsch Hoffert Cemetery in the company of my cousin Debbe, the one member of my mother's family with whom I've been able to connect. Yes, I was glad to have the opportunity to visit my great-grandparents' graves again without the pleas of my half-frozen family to pull me away, glad to admire again the wonderful simplicity of DAVID GREENBERG: POET, but that wasn't what I was really there for this time. It was Debbe who'd finally informed me, surprised at my ignorance—ah, but she didn't know that paternal line! its silent and silencing mottos—that here was where my mother, lost to me since infancy, was also buried, along with most of her immediate family.

And there they lay, as if gathered for one final family confab, that whole Fishman clan with the exception of sister Sophie, who'd gone off to live and die in Dayton with her husband, Marvin Schorr, no more than two rows away from David and Minnie. My mother, Bess Fishman Greenberg (1903–1932), her thin stone slab tilted slightly backward, like a cool, inviting headrest. On one side her parents, sharing a single large stone with middle-aged photographs of each of them on it: Morris (1867–1955), whom I'd visited once long ago in the Jewish Home for the Aged when he either couldn't or wouldn't communicate with me, and Anna (1865–1931), after whom I'd unknowingly named my own daughter, Ann. And on her other side, the four sisters who'd stayed in town with her: Jean (1900–1981), who'd married Joseph Klein, though it was my father who'd been expected to marry her after Bess's death; Rose (1897–1980), who'd married Louis Hart and joined Jean in sending me the birthday card that had briefly cracked open the whole mystery of this family's absence from my life; Minnie (1892–1935), who'd married Abe Bernstein; and Augusta (Gussie) (1888–1955), who'd married Harry Goldberg. All those people who'd been shut away from me all these years, whom my father had sunk deep in the icy lake of his silence, gathered here within easy hailing distance of David and Minnie Greenberg, no more than a whisper away, given the quiet of the cemetery that evening—not another visitor in sight on this occasion either—as if to welcome me home.

I paused there hand in hand with my cousin in the stillness of the summer evening, satisfied to have twice now found those I was looking for in this little cemetery, listening to their articulate silence, knowing it was not an end but a beginning.

## LOST AND FOUND

"My father is dead. My mother doesn't know who I am. My wife has left me. I don't know who I am anymore," whines famous juggler Michael Moschen (pronounced "Motion": what a wonderful name for a man whose occupation calls on him to keep objects in motion and who finds his very identity in flux) in a recent *New Yorker* article. But Michael Moschen, I want to tell him, *I* know who you are: You are a man whose father is dead, whose mother, an Alzheimer's patient, doesn't recognize him, and whose wife has left him. When it comes to the construction of identity, absence is as significant a marker as presence. If the deconstructionist mode has left us with anything of lasting value, surely it's in the understanding of how to read what's not there as carefully as what is there. Some of us, perhaps, have been looking for identity in all the wrong places.

Who am I, after all (though by no means, after all, all), but a man whose great-grandfather, a most uncommon literary ancestor, the poet and anarchist with whom he would have had so much in common, was deliberately and unceremoniously dumped into an open pit mine of family neglect that was quickly flooded with the waters of forgetfulness. Whose own mother, dead two months after his birth, was by paternal edict disappeared from the first two decades of his life. Whose first great love—though happily not his last—was killed by cancer. Yes, all of whose forebears are long since gone: the mother who raised him also by cancer, and his father, from whose memory he'd already slipped as if into nonexistence himself, from stroke and cancer and forgetfulness. Whose brother slips away now and then into misty alcoholic distances and whose three wonderful children, in the happier and more appropriate way of things, have grown up and gone off on their own, disappearing, as it were (though also still very much present), into their own lives.

And yet not for a moment would I say that "I don't know who I am anymore." Self-knowledge may be a dubious proposition at best, and my purpose here is certainly not to boast about or expatiate at great length upon my level of attainment of that slippery state, such as it is. But I do possess enough of it to know that who I am is defined not only by the nature and quality of the life I have now (which happens, if I may risk this precarious bit of immodesty about it—how often do we need to be reminded that whom the gods would destroy, they first make happy?—to be quite wonderful), but by all that has been taken away from me: by both the absences that once, like dark matter, filled so much of the little universe of my existence for so long and the now-gone presences like stars many light-years away who once burned brilliantly in my skies and still shine in my present though they've been long since extinguished.

Once upon a time, I used to think that loss was the only subject worth writing about. Eventually—with a little more self-awareness—I was able to revise that to say that loss was the only subject *I* could write about. Following that dismal recognition, I was able to blunder along to the next stage, which was to acknowledge that I had written about loss quite enough—poetry, fiction, essays, libretti, journals—and now it was time to commit myself to writing about anything but loss, to leave loss behind. Enough of loss, I told myself; on to something else, anything else. Ah yes, but what else, when almost every time I sat down to write what I found myself writing about (consciously or, just as frequently, not) was . . . loss? The order I'd so smartly given myself—Do not write about loss—proved to be much like that old, impossible-to-obey command: Do not think about elephants. Loss, I had to understand, *was* my subject. It was my elephant, as in that other old elephant joke: Where does an elephant sleep? It was impossible to shut the door against it.

Loss, after all, is one of life's great constants, beginning with the loss of the comfort and security of the womb and ending with the loss of life itself. In between, we lose our naïveté, our childlike wonder at the world, our virginity, varying chunks of our dreams and expectations, friends, lovers, dogs, keys, coins, extra pounds if we're lucky, our jobs or our minds if we're not, hair and teeth . . . the list goes on and on. There's nothing we have, no part of us (my tonsils, my appendix, my left kidney; occasionally my patience or my sense of humor; sadly, often someone near and dear to me), that we cannot lose. This is not news. I've lived with loss all my life, and so, in all likelihood, have you. What's intriguing about it here, especially for one who finds himself inescapably writing about it, is the extent to which it's loss, as much as anything else, possibly even as much as what we still have, that to a great extent defines us.

Loss, after all, is not a vessel we can empty, no matter how often we're required to drink from it. One never asks if the glass of loss is half empty or half full; it's always brimming over—or threatening to. Loss makes mockery of the parable of the loaves and fishes: no matter how much pours out, there is always more.

How it begins: When Wendy Parrish died, the tears came that I'd erected a barrier of busyness against while I tended to her needs during the final months of her decline from Hodgkin's disease. I cried. I wept. I flooded our yellow house with tears. I didn't know there could be so many tears or that so many had lain dammed up inside me. I wept all the tears I thought it was possible to weep, and then when I thought I'd poured them all out, that there couldn't possibly be any more in that deep, deep reservoir, that I had drained all the pools of tears inside me dry, I wept some more. I thought they would never stop flowing, though of course they did stop—I stopped them, plugged up that sea of tears with my heart filling the hole in the dike—when there were other people around. But as soon as I was alone, the dam burst again. This went on for days, for weeks. When I tried to salvage something of the day by going running through those bitter Minnesota January afternoons down boulevards empty of everything except ice and snow, the tears stopped me in vacant spaces, and I stood there wailing at the dark skies that bore down on me, pressing yet more tears out of my aching chest. Through tears icing my cheeks I screamed at the empty skies.

And if all this came slowly to an end as the months wore on, as the snow melted and the grass greened and the dying elms struggled to squeeze out their last few pale leaves and I began to allow a few people back into the empty chambers of my heart, it was, still, only a beginning. It was if I'd finally reached the bottom of that deep, deep well of tears, had bucket by bucket emptied it of every last drop, only to discover—even as my life meandered back onto something vaguely resembling its old, dry path—that there was no bottom, there was no emptying. It was as if I had learned not only that I was capable of pouring out such grief for this terrible loss, but also that I had, in the process, tapped some aquifer of loss and grief that anything, almost anything, could bring to the surface.

Many years later, my wife and I, only a few years married, were at the funeral of a fellow poet neither of us knew intimately. We were there not so much to honor the love or friendship that usually leads us to such places as to pay tribute to this man's life and work as a poet. It felt important, right, for us to be there, but not, as with a friend or loved one, as though it were a deep emotional event. I was, of course, as ignorant as ever. It took only one look at the poet's parents where they sat together in front of the coffin upraised on the altar for me to lose all composure, for the tears—tears of loss, any loss, all loss—to wash my face clean of any illusion that I could control such emotions, and, what's more, to suck my Janet right along with me into this powerful undertow of tears.

And now, as she well knows, I'm at risk in any movie, even for the occasional TV show, certainly for fiction, and not just for the scene of loss or unexpected joy there, but as much for the well-turned sentence, its revelation of knowledge or pain or beauty. I am reminded of how often, when I was a child, my father labeled me a crybaby, of how hard I must have labored for so many years to toughen myself against that charge, only to find out in later life not only how right he was—yes, I cried, I cry, I'll always cry—but how wrong he was as well. Ah, and so many years after my loss of him to recognize the likeness there: with this tough man who cried when he told me the ancient story of my mother's death, when he delivered me as a young draftee to the United States Army's processing center, when, aged (my own age now!), he said his good-byes to me at the Minneapolis–St. Paul airport, fearing he might never see me again . . . through whom also the rivers of loss flowed. Ah, what is this foolishness, I thought in those airport waiting rooms. Little did I know then.

■

Oh, I could give you a catalog of losses, though at my advancing age that should be no surprise to me or anyone else. After a certain point, we are all survivors. And yet they keep coming. Most recently my dearest friend and operatic collaborator, Eric Stokes, gone with the freeway's abrupt way of ending things, he who filled me and many others during his long career as a composer with the belief that, like people, "all sounds are innocent until proven guilty; . . . in their innocence they enjoy inalienable rights to proceed from any point of the compass, out of any height or depth however near or far as soever called forth by their composers or any other compelling life force." Only in Wendy, who had faced the threat of mortality early in her life, in her first bout with Hodgkin's, had I ever before seen such a passion for throwing one's arms around life; and there was Eric, saying the same thing over and over again in his notebooks in his own idiom: "Music sounds for the people. For all of us: the dumb, the deaf, the dogs & jays, the quick, handclappers, dancing moon watchers, brainy puzzlers, abstracted whistlers, finger snapping time keepers, crazy, weak, hurt, weed keepers, the strays. The land of music (everyone's nation) sounds in her tune, his beat, your drum—one song, one vote." And always, of course—as in the amazing music he wrote for *Apollonia's Circus,* our opera based on the Orpheus myth—a vote, finally, for life, its celebration in the face of all that is past and passing and to come: *Te morituri salutamus.*

This is where we continue to live, though, is it not? At death's door, which is apt to swing open for us at any moment, giving us yet another access to that many-roomed mansion of loss. Sometimes I try to convince myself that death should be written about from a distance, when there's been time to achieve some resolution to both the loss itself and one's own emotions. But then I find myself wandering through these rooms so filled with tangible absence that there's no backing away from it, no way to attain that distance. Absence is on my skin, in my hair and eyes and the palms of my hands, and I can no more let go of it than it's willing to let go of me. It's part of everything I am.

If there's one thing I found for myself in Wendy Parrish's all too early grasp of her own mortality, it's that absence is its own gift, blessing us with the value of the present, life in the here and now, a Stokesian enthusiasm for the music of his own life that still sings in my head. It's by no means all gloom in the house of absence. Absence is its own place, echoing with its own music: a lively, defining, resonant dwelling place, and no one should be ashamed or fearful of being a regular visitor there.

There's a phrase, a refrain, that still resonates within me from a long-ago reading of Paul Goodman's *Empire City:* "the presence of the absence of." This, if I remember Goodman correctly, is what we always live with, which is why he repeats the phrase so persistently throughout the novel. Yes, we live in the present, embedded as we need to be, as we cannot not be, as we must be if live we will, in the metropolis of our lives. But . . . no, make that "And." And absence lives there with us, in us, even, I would argue, for us: to let us know who and where we are, how much we're still defined by what we once found and loved and were loved by. If my father found it necessary to suppress my mother's very existence, as he did, that very suppression, the life he chose to live, was founded on his acknowledgment of her absence. Though he surely wouldn't have articulated it like this, her absence was every bit as much a part of him as her presence had been, a fact evidenced by the untapped wellspring of tears that burst from him when he at

long last told me the story of her death: the story that finally
made sense of the voids I'd felt all my young life. And if the
whole family conspired long ago to suppress the existence of
that anarchist-poet my great-grandfather, that absence, too,
like the live sacrifice some ancient cultures placed inside the
walls of new structures, became the core of the foundation on
which the family's future was erected, as my own generation's
recent excavations have discovered. Sometimes it takes a long
time to find what's missing, to read between the lines we've
inscribed in the books of our lives and understand how deeply
we're defined by what—and, more important, who—is no
longer there as we enter the later chapters.

They return to me in my dreams, of course: where I'm once
more in awe of Wendy's benevolence, where I return to work
with my father in his wine business, where Eric's laughing on
the phone again: "How are you, you old radical, you?" My
grandmother and stepmother show up as well from time to
time, and I'm sure my mother and great-grandfather would
visit me there too, if I'd had the chance to know them. They're
understanding, all of them; they never nag me, never demand

to know what I've done with the rest of my life since they departed; they move naturally through the long and often complex narratives of my sleeping self. They are, most often, just as they were in their lives: just as they continue to be in mine.

□

# VOICES

## A *Meditation*

Just when I thought I wouldn't be talking with the dead any longer, this voice comes up off the icy water and tells me, No way, no way am I going to shut him up. I look around and all I see is the other dog, the Irish setter, scouring the beach behind me, turning over rocks with her nose, looking for who-knows-what because it's too cold for life down here now. Near zero and a harsh wind etching the waters of the big lake, though otherwise it's calm, the water, that is, about as calm as this lake ever gets: some low, easy swells rolling across it now and then so that the lake moves like something breathing gently, sighing, softly raising and lowering the fine icing of ashes I've just scattered across its surface.

I'm hearing things, of course. Must be, because the setter, who'd otherwise never miss a squirrel scratching in a treetop halfway up the hill behind the beach, is still snuffling around among the rocks. She has no more interest in what I'm doing down here than she does in what's happening on the far shore, fifty miles away, lost to sight over the horizon. Either that, I'm thinking, or she's decided that if I'm going to carry on this sort of conversation, for real or not, she wants no part of it. I know, I know, I credit animals with too much volition. This voice I'm hearing, for example. But in all this brightness, this perfectly cloudless sky and midday winter sun shimmering off the lake, the setter keeps her nose fixed to the ground. Whatever I'm about, she wants nothing to do with it.

This is November. This is the season when Lake Superior throws its worst at the world: storms that rip beach houses off their foundations, storms that snatch sailors off the decks of their ships and drive oceangoing freighters onto the rocks, storms that reshape lives and landscapes. They take my beach away one November and bring it back the next. Even today, calm as you're ever likely to see it except for maybe a week in the middle of July, you'd have to admit that the slow inhale-exhale of its movement is the breathing of a sleeping giant. I'm not fooled, and that wind, which must be what's bringing tears to the corners of my eyes, tells me I'm right not to be fooled. And then there's that voice.

Talking to the dead isn't so far-fetched as it sounds, you know. There are plenty of other cultures around the world, in fact, where it's simply taken for granted that the dead continue their conversations with us. I'm no spiritualist, though. I'm just your basic American white guy, which is to confess that I have the heart of a pragmatist and the soul of a realist. One of my first memories is of jabbing my baby cousin through the bars of her crib to challenge the sudden reality of her appearance in my world. The prospective scientist at work, forming a tentative hypothesis and testing it. This methodology I quickly understood to possess great power because of the spanking it promptly brought down upon me. The gods, as I later came to understand, punish us most severely not for the falsehoods we invent but for the truths we discover.

Here, I don't yet know what the truth is, or even who the gods of the moment are, but I do know there are things still to be learned. I have never been one to shrug off what other people say just because it doesn't happen to coincide with my own vision of the world. You never can tell is what I always say. At any moment the impossible is apt to slide up over the horizon like a midnight sunrise, and if you're not prepared for it, what then? This is not the sort of thing I would ordinarily admit, because I also think life can be harder on you than it need be if you don't keep the integrity of your approach to it intact, for the sake of those around you as well as yourself. But you have also got to realize that just because certain things exist outside the boundaries of your vision doesn't mean they're not there to be seen. Sometime. By someone. Or heard.

Here is my ceremony: I stand at the very edge of the water, on a slope of small stones clad in ice and threatening at any moment to slide out from under me, to slide me into the water. I hold in my hands a green plastic bag, about as big as a two-pound bag of sugar, surprisingly heavy for its size. I take off my woolen gloves. Ceremonies, as I understand them, must be hands-on experiences: the knife on the foreskin, the ring on the finger, the shovelful of dirt. I stuff my gloves in the pockets of my down jacket and slowly untwist the wire that closes the top of the plastic bag. I put the wire and the cardboard identification tag attached to it in one of those pockets. I spread the neck of the bag open and dip my right hand into its contents, surprised, when I lift it out, at how light the gray-white handful of powder and chips feels, after the weight of the full bag. I cast this handful out toward the lake, and as the ashes drift out over the water some of them blow back toward the shore in the swirling winds. Most of them settle on the water, like leaves, or pollen, too light to sink, riding the easy swells. Some dust the icy rocks at my feet. Others blow back onto me, onto my blue jacket, where they cling like dandruff, like part of me. Into my beard, I'm sure. The ceremony continues. I cast handful after handful of ashes upon the lake, until the bag is empty, and then turn the bag itself upside down and shake it, while the wind goes on doing its windy things. I stuff the empty bag in my pocket but still stand there, watching the ashes that coat the surface of the water.

I'm not quite finished. I have a few things to say. Ceremonies need their words as well as their gestures, and even though I don't expect them to be heard, I will say them aloud. Words of gratitude, history, farewell. Then this ceremony will come to an end. But there's something I don't understand. Ceremonies, of course, are the bonds of civilization, the occasions by which we identify our group selves, and celebrate that identification. That this is a ceremony I have no doubt. But what am I to make of its solitary nature? Of the fact that I engage in it alone, my only companion a red-haired dog that pays no attention to me, to it, that shows more interest in ice-encrusted rocks than my warm-blooded presence? With what or whom, I wonder, am I to bond, identify, celebrate here, on the edge of this awesome body of frigid water? And then I hear the voice.

Probably no one has more of value to say to us than the dead, who finally have the Archimedean stance we have always longed for, the leverage to lift and weigh the world, and no reason to give us false measure, though just how forthcoming they're willing to be probably depends more on us than on them: our patience, our expectations. This is the difference between the fact that, as Sonny says, they will not be shut up, and our own choice of whether or not to listen. They know as well as anyone that anytime you start to tell a story, your listener is perfectly free to put down his drink and walk away, and therefore they—the smart ones at least, and, in spite of what some say, old Sonny is surely one of those—know enough to establish ceremonial beginnings, rituals that instantly cement community, that we cannot walk away from. "Once upon a time," they say, and who can turn his back on that?

Even as he tells it I recall every moment of it, intimately, sensuously. I'm not even sure I'm listening to what he's saying, so caught up am I in the physical details of memory, the things for which there are no words. Is anyone even talking? I don't need words. The ceremony has begun. Again. Once I was an observer. Then I became an initiate. A participant. Someday I shall be its priest. The words shall be mine. And you shall be my congregation. You will stand beside the shore, in freezing temperatures and a vicious wind, and listen to what I have to say. You will not be able to turn away. You will not even want to turn away. You will scatter your own life on this wind, these waters, and it will blow back to you, in a voice you barely recognize. But what you will recognize is the need to listen to it, the importance of not shutting it up, no matter how unlikely you think even its very presence, the fact that there is no telling how the world may finally choose to speak to you, that only by your good graces can the word, the all-important word, come home.

It should be no surprise to me that when it comes it doesn't stand on ceremony. It sounds, if anything, a little grumpy. It rolls up from under the whine of the wind in the birches and balsams behind me. It rumbles through the midrange of my own mutterings. I have just finished acknowledging this entire decade, which is itself on the verge of slipping into its grave. For the next month or two people will occupy themselves with trying to define the eighties, but for me the decade's already defined by this big, yellow Lab who came to me at the beginning of it and now leaves me at the end. The eighties were Sonny's years, he who was my most constant companion, and the nineties will have to be something else. But this is the end of the eighties, I am saying into the wind that ricochets off the hard, cold, smooth waters and snaps at my face, my eyes. The eighties are over. This is the last we will hear of the eighties.

Then I hear the voice, as slow and deep as I always imagined it would be coming out of that great barrel chest.

It says, Wanna bet?

Grandmother, mother, lover: until today the voices have always been female. And in most ways they have all been one voice, the voice of consolation, telling me what I needed to hear even when I didn't know I needed to hear it: that I am loved. They have been gentle, solemn voices, necessary voices but quiet ones, whispering directly into my ear, the hush of their assurances more important than their particular words. I think they are voices like this lake today—rare, slow moving, deep, and finally impenetrable, or entered, fully, only with the knowledge that they will never be left again. They are the voices whose task is to turn me, still, back to the shore, and I have learned to listen to them, though at times it's taken great effort to do so, not to want to hear them as the siren songs they never meant themselves to be.

But this is the gruff male voice of a swimmer. Grace of a seal in water. The raised head and the smooth, steady strokes. Deep lungs and webbed paws. The oily undercoat that repels the cold, sheds the wet. Ready to plunge back in at the slightest enticement. And this is *his* lake. What does he want of me?

Once, years ago, later in the season than this, February maybe, the whole little bay here was frozen over, and the lake itself, too, as far as the eye could see, covered roughly with great wind-thrust chunks of blue ice, some of them chest high, sharp edged, swept clean of snow. Your classic moonscape, and you only ventured onto it as cumbersomely clad as an astronaut. One afternoon I walked out there—or climbed, was more like it, scrambling over those huge blocks of ice, sliding, falling, the wind at its work as usual, a fine snowfall sifting almost sideways over the ice, and the whole great thing I walked on creaking and groaning under me. Whether it would hold or not, or crack open and dump me weighted down with thermal underwear and sweaters and jeans and jacket and hat and scarf and gloves into the icy waters below, I neither knew nor cared. The sounds were threatening, but I didn't feel threatened, not even when I'd made my slow way well out beyond the mouth of the bay and onto the lake itself, where I stood on a glassy-floored valley among hills of ice and suddenly saw, looking back and wondering what the chances were of a split developing that would cut me off from shore, Sonny's head peering at me over a block of ice.

Not a word from him then. Not a bark or a growl or a whine. Just those big amber eyes in that big, yellow head. All right, I said, I'm coming.

This is the kind of place where you can't stay very long. Even with the lake calm, the wind light, the temperature, well, still above zero at least, there's something about it that tells you not to linger. Nothing seems to be happening, but, still, it's too intense, and we can take only just so much intensity. The setter has wandered back off the beach, among the trees, where she's scratching up the snow and earth at the foot of a birch, uncovering, so far as I can see, nothing. On the other hand, intensity is like a stake through the chest. It pins you there and you are motionless, awestruck simply at the fact that such a thing could be happening. You could pull it out, of course, but what then? How could you live with the gaping wound of its absence? Where would you go when it let loose of you?

A voice can be just like that. A dream. When she comes back to me in the middle of the night, I know there is a part of me that never wants to wake up, just as I also know that dreams are not places where we can ever, ever, linger for very long. And despite what I once thought, as their frequency seemed to diminish somewhat over the decade following her death, we are never done with them, either. They simply come, unbidden, unexpected, always intense. We have shaken off the daily dust, wiped our hands, begun to turn away, and there, suddenly, it is. A voice off the moving waters. The setter turns, beneath the birch, to look out toward the lake, lifts her head, sniffs, I think, the wind. I call her name, and she begins to circle toward me, warily, in a wide arc, over the icy stones of the beach. She is not even my dog, but my daughter's, but I have brought her along—borrowed her, as it were—as a necessary and proper companion for this occasion. She and Sonny always got along just fine. Me, I think, she's less certain about, even though now she nudges her big head under my woolen hand. Surely, except for the familiar comfort of being scratched behind her ears, she finds this all very strange. She's not alone in that.

It takes just such a voice as this, in fact, to remind us that we're never alone. I'm not talking spirits, understand; this is the voice of the realist, remember, the materialist, if you prefer. Animism just isn't my line, much as I find it an attractive and appealing way of being in and with this world and all its parts, animate and inanimate alike, though I guess the very point of such a belief is that the whole world *is* animate in all its parts. An appealing notion, indeed, as well as one that has led some cultures to take far better care of the world than we seem prone to doing. I often wish I could be more than merely wistful about it.

And then I hear this voice. Do I know where it comes from? What I know is it's here. Do I know whose it is? Without a doubt. Do I listen to it? To quote the voice itself: You bet. But it isn't easy to come up with what it's saying—no more than it's possible to recite the true nature of a dream, however well you can relate some of its images as they fly past you in the night. These things are here, and their point is simply that: their *hereness.* Maybe, after all, the fact is that in spite of their advantageous position, the dead don't really have anything to tell us. Not, that is, the sort of stuff we've always thought we'd like to have them reveal: What's it like on the other side? What's the meaning of life? Is there, you know, a god? Did you really mean to leave me out of the will?

Well, yes, I can see that if it's *hereness* I want, this Irish setter is very definitely here. She is sitting on the rocks very patiently beside me where I stand, and she is very impatiently insisting that I continue scratching her behind her ears. That's presence for you. And that, after all, is what I brought her along for—her presence. She's good at that, presence, as the animals I have known always seem to be: when they're there, they're there. Unlike some people. But what I think this voice is telling me, these voices have told me—not in so many words, you understand—is simply that what, or who, has once been here is always here. Someone may go, but the presence remains. At least so long as someone is listening to it, for it. I don't want to get into that silly tree-in-the-forest issue; who cares? The fact is, *I* hear it. Them. What else counts?

■

Some it takes a long time to learn to listen for—or perhaps to learn that that's what you're hearing. My mother died when I was born. To reiterate that long story briefly, since the afternoon is waning, shadows have completely captured the beach now, and a harsher wind is scraping across rock and water, no one told me. The reasons for this are as arbitrary as anything else in life, as arbitrary as the reason for her death (delivery-room sepsis in the preantibiotic age), though when I think about the conspiracy of silence that ensued, the energies it must have taken to suppress her very existence for the next two decades, I am still dumbfounded: they could have powered so much else. Perhaps that was some of the energy that was suddenly unleashed when the uncovering of this secret sent the earth spinning beneath my feet.

There was a dog by my side then, too, an aging black-and-white cocker spaniel lying quietly at my feet, peering out the picture window at the spring-green grasses in the backyard, the afternoon sunlight splashing through the oaks, the busy squirrels. Coming out of that dizzying moment, I suddenly felt as if everything had finally fallen into place. Same room, dog, house, city, etcetera, but now for the first time, thanks to one piece of accidentally acquired information—but what information!—everything began to make a sort of sense, all the oddities of nearly two decades of my life, all that had been struggling to come to the surface to say to me that the multitude of little things that had never made sense to me all those years would, would, if only . . .

And there, finally, was the "if only." A resurrection, if you want. A presence restored. The only presence that could begin to make some sense of that world. A presence that had struggled to reveal itself to me, in my childish ignorance and confusion—for the signs were there, if I'd only known how to attend, to listen to them (that there *was* something to listen for!)—for so long. A presence that would not be denied. A presence not to be denied. And it didn't matter what was said. All that mattered was that she was there.

■

As I turn away from the beach, pausing to take one last look out over the lake, what I don't expect to see taking shape like the fog that so often materializes just above water level—that in a matter of minutes can take on thickness and density, become a frighteningly tangible force, blotting out anything a dozen feet away, lake or shoreline or trees—is the gradually coalescing shape of a big, yellow dog with ears too small for his head and an appetite too big for his body. This may be a grade-B life, but it's not a grade-B movie, not some TV horror flick with its midnight muddle of mysterious manifestations. There was nothing mysterious about Sonny, nothing wraith-like about that appetite, that bulk or bark. I do not expect to see his like again. Or hers. Or my grandmother's. Or my mother's, whom I never did see. But I expect their presences always. To listen to them: because whatever they say or don't say, their presence alone makes the statement most needed. This, I realize, is the community I was wondering about earlier. This is what my ceremony has given me.

And yes, I tell myself, as I leave the beach and lake behind and start up the narrow, woodsy path to the house, the red dog trailing at my heels, my boots leaving fresh footprints in the light snow, for the wind has covered up the old ones, yes, even his. Not Sonny's this time, but the presence I've been having the hardest time granting admittance to here: my father's. For a moment longer I try to suppress this urge as I trudge through the little ravine below the house. The sky has darkened rapidly, not just the cloud cover sliding in out of the east, across the lake, presaging storm, but the onrushing early twilight of November, tumbling downhill toward the solstice. The wind off the lake, funneled through the ravine, hustles me along the path. Quickly, then, before the last push up the hill out of the ravine and the snow and wind and cold and into the bright lights and fireplace warmth and ease of the house. All right, I'll have him too. Even though he was the one who managed, insisted on, the suppression of my mother's existence for all those years, I'll have his presence here now too. His voice. Yes, I could hear it, too. But in fact, and not surprisingly, he doesn't speak. Doesn't even say thanks. Just looks at me with his dark eyes and nods. It's okay, Pops. Everyone belongs.

At the top of the hill, the setter bounds in front of me to the door of the house, where she stands waiting, wagging her long, raggedy red tail. Sonny, I imagine, would be stopping by the side of the path just behind me to pee one last time and, in that deep voice, mumbling something like, "Wait up."

"You bet," I'd tell him. "Anytime."

## ABOUT THE ILLUSTRATIONS

Page 34–The author's biological mother, Bess Greenberg.

Page 44–(*left to right*) The author's uncle Ed, aunt Ethyl, and father Herb, circa 1928–1929, Miami Beach or its vicinity.

Page 116–David Greenberg, the author's great-grandfather, circa 1900–1910.

Page 120–The David Greenberg family (left to right): Bertha (b. 1878), David (b. 1853), Abram (b. 1876), Benjamin (the author's grandfather, b. 1881), and Minnie (b. 1856).

Page 168–Family headstones at the Hirsch Hoffert Cemetery.

Page 176–The grave of Wendy Parrish.

## ABOUT THE AUTHOR

Courtesy Robert Meier

Alvin Greenberg is the author of three novels and several collections of short stories and of poetry, including *Why We Live with Animals*. His most recent book is the collection of stories *How the Dead Live*. He lives in Boise, Idaho.